quilts made with love

To Celebrate, Comfort, and Show You Care

Rachel Griffith

Martingale®
Create with Confidence

Dedication

To my children, Jackson, Melanie, Andrew, and Lindsey—everything I do, I do for y'all. Including this book. Here's proof that dreams do come true if y'all are willing to work for them. And I expect y'all to dream big.
Love, Mom.

Quilts Made with Love:
To Celebrate, Comfort, and Show You Care
© 2013 by Rachel Griffith

Martingale®
19021 120th Ave. NE, Ste. 102
Bothell, WA 98011-9511 USA
ShopMartingale.com

Printed in China
18 17 16 15 14 13   8 7 6 5 4 3 2 1

Library of Congress Cataloging-in-Publication Data is available upon request.

ISBN: 978-1-60468-289-2

Mission Statement

Dedicated to providing quality products and service to inspire creativity.

Credits

President and CEO: Tom Wierzbicki
Editor in Chief: Mary V. Green
Design Director: Paula Schlosser
Managing Editor: Karen Costello Soltys
Acquisitions Editor: Karen M. Burns
Technical Editor: Nancy Mahoney
Copy Editor: Sheila Chapman Ryan
Production Manager: Regina Girard
Cover and Interior Designer: Regina Girard
Photographer: Brent Kane
Illustrator: Rose Wright

contents

Introduction   5

quilts to celebrate

Bitsy Baby   8
Hopscotch and Ribbons   11
Sweet Cheeks   15
All Together Now   18
Oh Happy Day   21
Pathways   24
It Takes Two   27
Unconditional   31
No Place Like Home   34
Happily Ever After   38
Around the Block   41

quilts to comfort

Farsighted   46
Look to the Stars   48
Second Wind   52
Epilogue   56
Turnaround   59
Heartfelt   62
Sincerely   65
Embrace   68

Quiltmaking Basics   73
Acknowledgments   79
About the Author   80

Quilters are generally known as loving people. We make quilts for almost every occasion, good or bad.

In happy times, we make quilts to celebrate marriages, new homes, and babies. In unhappy times, we make quilts for cancer patients, widows, and families affected by natural disasters like fires, floods, and tornados.

As quilters, we know the sense of satisfaction when we present someone with a beautiful quilt. But when we give a much-needed quilt—a quilt that touches the heart—everyone feels the love that covers and surrounds that particular quilt. Although we may not always be selfless with our hobby, it's a wonderful feeling when we share our love by giving away something we've labored over.

So whether you've chosen this book to make quilts of celebration or quilts of comfort, know that a quilt is a timeless, outward sign of caring . . . a way to celebrate, a way to comfort, and a way to show we care.

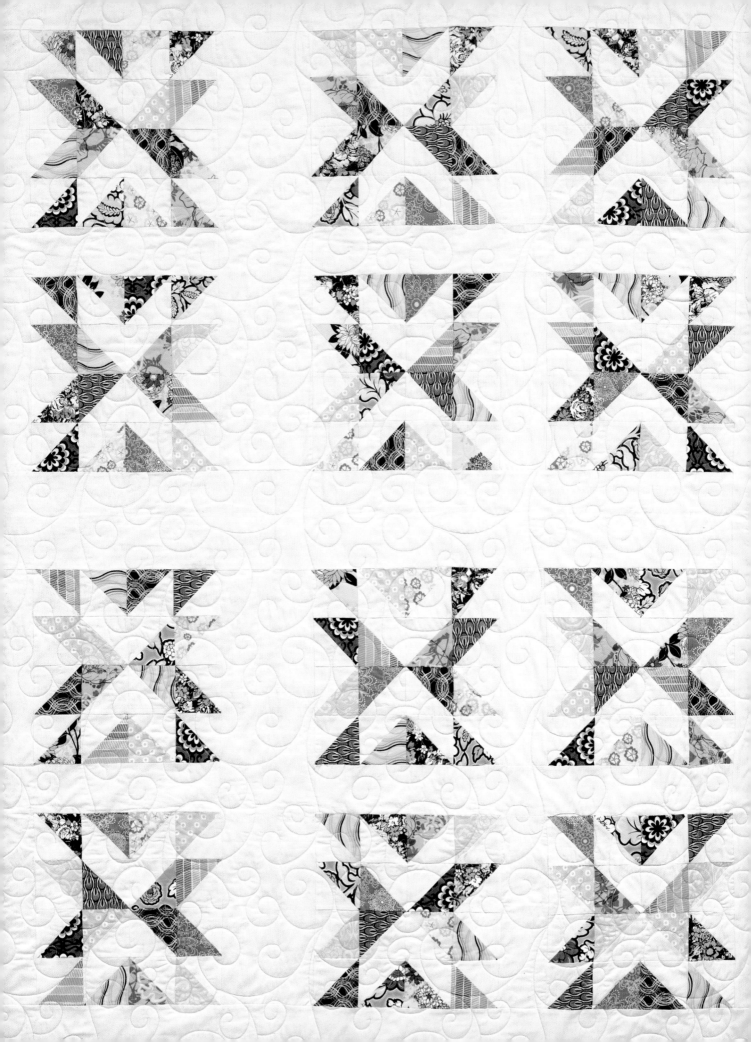

bitsy baby

Simple and sweet for your favorite little guy. I love this quilt for its traditional yet modern feel. It's perfect for using those special little bits in your stash that you don't want to throw away.

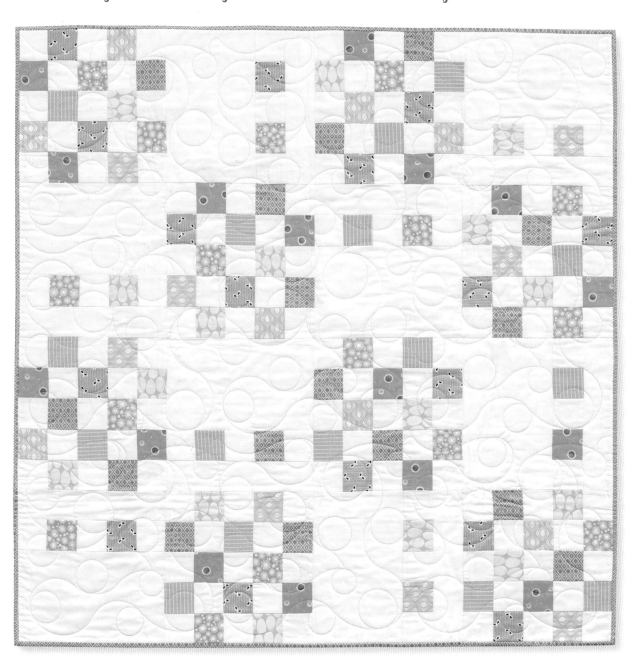

Finished quilt: 40½" x 40½" • Finished block: 10" x 10"

Designed by Rachel Griffith; pieced by Molly Culley; quilted by Darla Padilla.

materials

Yardage is based on 42"-wide fabric unless otherwise specified.

7 strips, 2½" x 42", of assorted prints for blocks
1⅜ yards of white solid for blocks
½ yard of fabric for binding
2⅔ yards of fabric for backing
45" x 45" piece of batting

cutting

From *each* of the 2½"-wide strips, cut:
⊕ 16 squares, 2½" x 2½" (112 squares total)

From the white solid, cut:
⊕ 8 strips, 2½" x 42"; crosscut into 128 squares, 2½" x 2½"
⊕ 2 strips, 10½" x 42"; crosscut into:
    8 rectangles, 2½" x 10½"
    8 rectangles, 6½" x 10½"

From the binding fabric, cut:
⊕ 5 strips, 2¼" x 42"

making the postage stamp blocks

1. Lay out 12 assorted print squares and 13 white squares, alternating the print and white squares as shown. Join the squares into rows. Press the seam allowances toward the print squares. Join the rows to make a Postage Stamp block. Press the seam allowances in one direction.

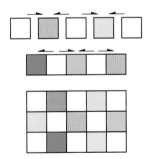

2. Repeat to make a total of eight Postage Stamp blocks, 10½" square.

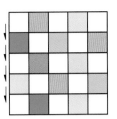

Postage Stamp block.
Make 8.

making the strip blocks

1. Join two assorted print squares and three white squares, alternating the squares as shown to make a strip set. Press the seam allowances toward the print squares.

2. Sew a white 2½" x 10½" rectangle to the right side of the strip set and a white 6½" x 10½" rectangle to the left side of the strip set. Press the seam allowances toward the just-added rectangles.

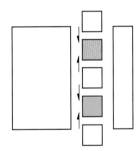

3. Repeat to make a total of eight Strip blocks, 10½" square.

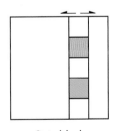

Strip block.
Make 8.

assembling the quilt top

1. Lay out the Postage Stamp blocks and Strip blocks in four rows of four blocks each, alternating the blocks as shown below.
2. Sew the blocks together in rows. Press the seam allowances toward the Strip blocks.
3. Sew the rows together. Press the seam allowances in one direction.

finishing the quilt

For detailed instructions on finishing techniques, refer to "Quiltmaking Basics" on pages 76–78. Use the 2¼"-wide strips to make and attach the binding.

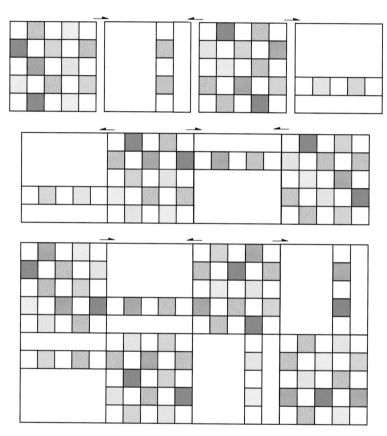

Quilt assembly

hopscotch and ribbons

Little girls love hopscotch and ribbons. And they're sure to love this quilt. This is a great quilt to showcase your favorite prints.

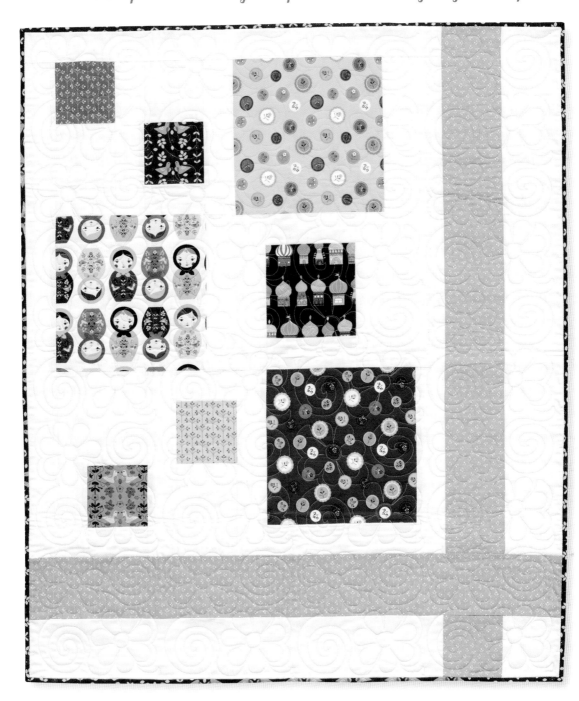

Finished quilt: 36½" x 42½"

Designed and pieced by Rachel Griffith; quilted by Darla Padilla.
Fabrics featured are Little Kukla by Suzy Altman for Robert Kaufman Fabrics.

materials

Yardage is based on 42"-wide fabric unless otherwise specified.

¾ yard *total* of bright-colored scraps, no smaller than 5" x 5"

1⅛ yards of white solid

⅜ yard of green print for borders

½ yard of fabric for binding

2⅜ yards of fabric for backing

41" x 47" piece of batting

cutting

From the bright-colored scraps, cut *a total of*:
- 4 squares, 4½" x 4½"
- 1 square, 6½" x 6½"
- 3 squares, 10½" x 10½"

From the white solid, cut:
- 3 strips, 2½" x 4½"
- 2 strips, 2½" x 6½"
- 3 strips, 2½" x 10½"
- 4 strips, 2½" x 12½"
- 1 strip, 2½" x 28½"
- 1 strip, 2½" x 32½"
- 2 squares, 4½" x 4½"
- 3 strips, 4½" x 6½"
- 2 strips, 4½" x 10½"
- 1 strip, 4½" x 28½"
- 1 strip, 4½" x 34½"
- 1 strip, 6½" x 10½"

From the green print, cut:
- 1 strip, 4½" x 34½"
- 1 strip, 4½" x 36½"
- 1 square, 4½" x 4½"

From the binding fabric, cut:
- 5 strips, 2¼" x 42"

making the rows

1. For row 1, join a white 4½" x 6½" strip to a bright 4½" square. Join a white 4½" square to a bright 4½" square, and then add a white 2½" x 4½" strip. Press the seam allowances toward the bright squares.

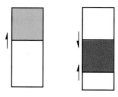

2. Lay out the units from step 1, two white 2½" x 10½" strips, one bright 10½" square, and one white 4½" x 10½" strip as shown. Join the pieces to complete row 1. Press the seam allowances in the directions indicated.

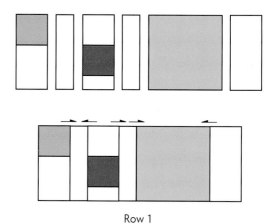

Row 1

3. For row 2, join the white 2½" x 6½" strips to opposite sides of the bright 6½" square. Press the seam allowances toward the bright square.

4. Lay out one bright 10½" square, one white 4½" x 10½" strip, the unit from step 3, and the white 6½" x 10½" strip as shown. Join the pieces to complete row 2. Press the seam allowances in the direction indicated.

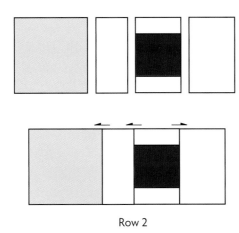

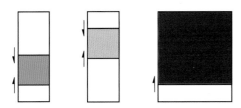

Row 2

5. For row 3, join a white 4½" x 6½" strip to a bright 4½" square, and then add a white 2½" x 4½" strip. Repeat to make a second unit. Join a bright 10½" square and a white 2½" x 10½" strip. Press the seam allowances toward the bright squares.

6. Lay out the units from step 5 and four white 2½" x 12½" strips as shown. Join the pieces to complete row 3. Press the seam allowances in the direction indicated.

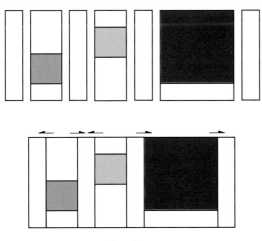

Row 3

assembling the quilt top

1. Lay out the three rows as shown. Join the rows to complete the quilt center. Press the seam allowances in one direction.

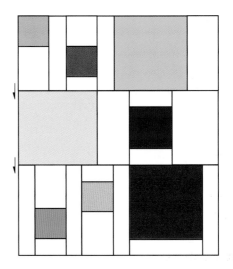

2. Sew the white 2½" x 32½" strip to the left side and the white 2½" x 28½" strip to the top of the quilt center as shown in the quilt assembly diagram on page 14. Press the seam allowances toward the white strips.

3. Join the white 4½" x 28½" strip to the green 4½" square, and then add a white 4½" square. Press the seam allowances toward the green square.

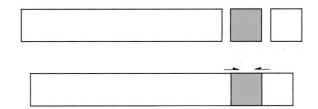

4. Join the green 4½" x 34½" strip to the white 4½" x 34½" strip to complete the side border. Press the seam allowances toward the green strip.

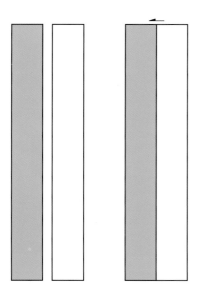

5. Add the border strip from step 4 to the right side of the quilt center and press the seam allowances toward the green strip. Join the green 4½" x 36½" strip to the bottom of the quilt center, and then add the border from step 3 on page 13 to complete the quilt top. Press the seam allowances toward the green strips.

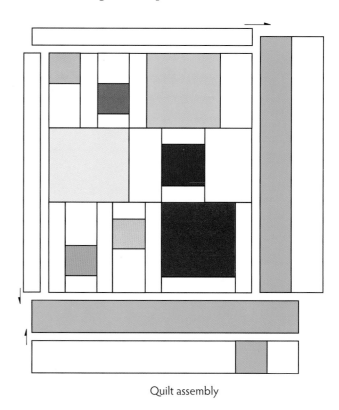

Quilt assembly

finishing the quilt

For detailed instructions on finishing techniques, refer to "Quiltmaking Basics" on pages 76–78. Use the 2¼"-wide strips to make and attach the binding.

sweet cheeks

This is my go-to baby quilt when I need a shower gift. It's perfect for both boys and girls, comes together quickly, and is oh-so sweet.

Finished quilt: 36½" x 36½"

Designed and pieced by Rachel Griffith; quilted by Darla Padilla.
Fabrics featured are Odds and Ends by Julie Comstock for Moda Fabrics.

materials

Yardage is based on 42"-wide fabric unless otherwise specified.

10 fat eighths (9" x 21") of assorted prints for small block and rectangles

2 fat quarters (18" x 21") of assorted prints for large block

½ yard of aqua print for large block

1 scrap, at least 5" x 5", of print for small block

⅜ yard of fabric for binding

2½ yards of fabric for backing

41" x 41" piece of batting

cutting

From 1 fat quarter, cut:
❀ 1 square, 8½" x 8½"

From the remaining fat quarter, cut:
❀ 2 strips, 4½" x 8½"
❀ 2 strips, 4½" x 16½"

From the print scrap, cut:
❀ 1 square, 4½" x 4½"

From *each of 8* fat eighths, cut:
❀ 1 strip, 6½" x 12½" (8 total)

From 1 fat eighth, cut:
❀ 2 strips, 2½" x 4½"
❀ 2 strips, 2½" x 8½"

From the remaining fat eighth, cut:
❀ 2 strips, 2½" x 8½"
❀ 2 strips, 2½" x 12½"

From the aqua print, cut:
❀ 2 strips, 4½" x 16½"
❀ 2 strips, 4½" x 24½"

From the binding fabric, cut:
❀ 4 strips, 2¼" x 42"

making the large block

1. Sew the assorted 4½" x 8½" strips to opposite sides of the assorted 8½" square. Press the seam allowances toward the strips. Sew the matching 4½" x 16½" strips to the top and bottom edges of the unit. Press the seam allowances toward the just-added strips.

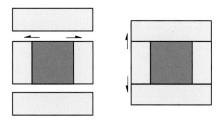

2. Sew the aqua 4½" x 16½" strips to opposite sides of the center unit. Press the seam allowances toward the aqua strips. Sew the aqua 4½" x 24½" strips to the top and bottom edges to complete the block. Press the seam allowances toward the just-added strips.

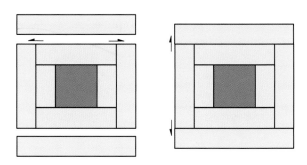

making the small block

1. Sew the assorted 2½" x 4½" strips to opposite sides of the 4½" square. Press the seam allowances toward the strips. Sew the matching 2½" x 8½" strips to the top and bottom edges of the unit. Press the seam allowances toward the just-added strips.

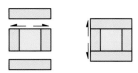

2. Sew the assorted 2½" x 8½" strips to opposite sides of the center unit. Press the seam allowances toward the just-added strips. Sew the matching 2½" x 12½" strips to the top and bottom edges to complete the block. Press the seam allowances toward the just-added strips.

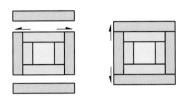

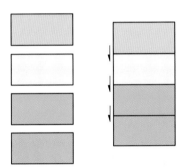

assembling the quilt top

1. Join four assorted 6½" x 12½" rectangles side by side to make a rectangular unit. Press the seam allowances in one direction. Repeat to make a second rectangular unit.

2. Lay out the large block, small block, and the two rectangular units as shown in the quilt assembly diagram below.

3. Sew the blocks and units together into rows. Press the seam allowances toward the blocks. Then join the rows to complete the quilt top. Press the seam allowances in one direction.

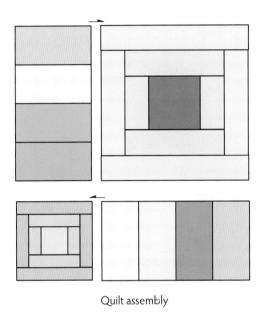

Quilt assembly

finishing the quilt

For detailed instructions on finishing techniques, refer to "Quiltmaking Basics" on pages 76–78. Use the 2¼"-wide strips to make and attach the binding.

all together now

Adopting a child is exciting for the whole family. Using stash fabrics to make a scrappy quilt can be a special gesture symbolizing a "pieced" or blended family.

Finished quilt: 56½" x 56½" • Finished block: 14" x 14"

Designed by Rachel Griffith; pieced by Molly Culley; quilted by Darla Padilla.

materials

Yardage is based on 42"-wide fabric unless otherwise specified.

24 squares, 5" x 5", of assorted aqua prints for blocks

24 squares, 5" x 5", of assorted green prints for blocks

24 squares, 5" x 5", of assorted red prints for blocks

24 squares, 5" x 5", of assorted yellow prints for blocks

2 yards of white solid for blocks

⅝ yard of fabric for binding

3¾ yards of fabric for backing

61" x 61" piece of batting

cutting

Set aside 16 squares of each assorted color (64 total.)

From the *remaining* assorted 5" squares, cut:

- 128 squares, 2" x 2" (32 of each color)

From the white solid, cut:

- 21 strips; 3" x 42"; crosscut into:
    - 64 rectangles, 3" x 5"
    - 64 rectangles, 3" x 7½"

From the binding fabric, cut:

- 7 strips, 2¼" x 42"

making the units

1. Draw a line from corner to corner on the wrong side of each assorted 2" square. With right sides together, place a marked square on one end of a white 3" x 5" rectangle as shown. Sew on the marked line. Trim away the corner fabric, leaving a ¼"-wide seam allowance. Press the seam allowances open. Make 64 units.

Make 64.

2. With right sides together, place a marked square on one end of a white 3" x 7½" rectangle as shown. In the same manner as before, sew on the marked line, trim, and press to make 64 of these units.

Make 64.

3. Lay out one of the 5" squares, one unit from step 1, and one unit from step 2 as shown. Sew the shorter unit to the square. Press the seam allowances open. Add the longer unit and press the seam allowances open. Repeat the process to make a total of 64 units.

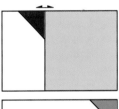

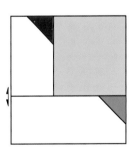

Make 64.

making the blocks

Lay out four units as shown, making sure the square in each unit is a different color. Join the units into rows. Press the seam allowances to one side. Join the rows and press the seam allowances in one direction. Repeat to make a total of 16 blocks.

assembling the quilt top

1. Lay out the blocks in four rows of four blocks each. Sew the blocks together into rows. Press the seam allowances in opposite directions from row to row.
2. Sew the rows together. Press the seam allowances in one direction.

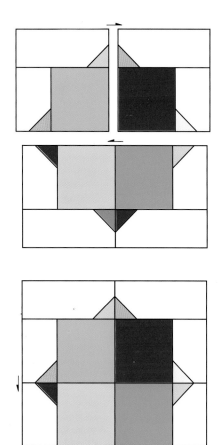

Make 16.

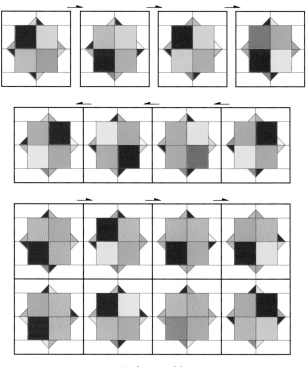

Quilt assembly

finishing the quilt

For detailed instructions on finishing techniques, refer to "Quiltmaking Basics" on pages 76–78. Use the 2¼"-wide strips to make and attach the binding.

oh happy day

Your family and friends deserve to be celebrated on their birthday. Do it with a quilt. I love that this quilt can easily be adapted to the recipient's taste and favorite colors.

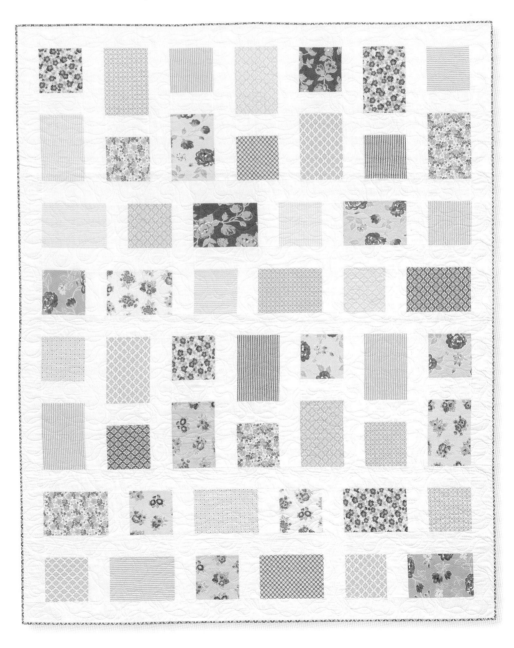

Finished quilt: 66½" x 81½" • Finished block: 6" x 18"
Designed by Rachel Griffith; pieced by Molly Culley; quilted by Darla Padilla.
Fabrics featured are Marmalade by Bonnie and Camille for Moda Fabrics.

materials

Yardage is based on 42"-wide fabric unless otherwise specified.

26 fat eighths (9" x 21") of assorted prints for blocks

3⅛ yards of white solid for blocks, sashing, and border

⅝ yard of fabric for binding

5¼ yards of fabric for backing

70" x 85" piece of batting

cutting

From *each* of the assorted prints, cut:

✤ 1 square, 6½" x 6½" (26 total)

✤ 1 rectangle, 6½" x 9½" (26 total)

From the white solid, cut:

✤ 16 strips, 3½" x 42"; crosscut into:
  18 strips, 3½" x 18½"
  4 strips, 3½" x 15½"
  26 strips, 3½" x 6½"

✤ 13 strips, 3½" x 42"

From the binding fabric, cut:

✤ 8 strips, 2¼" x 42".

making the strip blocks

1. Join a print 6½" square and a white 3½" x 6½" strip as shown. Press the seam allowances toward the square. Repeat to make a total of 26 units.

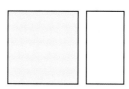

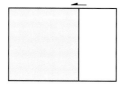

Make 26.

2. Sew a print 6½" x 9½" rectangle to the other side of the white strip as shown. Press the seam allowances toward the print strip. Repeat to make a total of 26 Strip blocks.

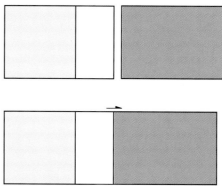

Make 26.

assembling the quilt top

1. Lay out six Strip blocks, three white 3½" x 18½" strips, and two white 3½" x 15½" strips as shown. Join blocks to both sides of each horizontal strip and press the seam allowances toward the blocks. Then join the block units and vertical strips to complete row A. Press the seam allowances toward the block units. The row should measure 66½" long. Repeat to make a second row A.

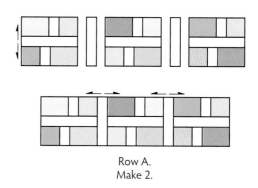

Row A.
Make 2.

2. Lay out seven Strip blocks and six white 3½" x 18½" strips, rotating the blocks as shown. Join the blocks and strips to make row B. Press the seam allowances toward the blocks. The row should measure 66½" long. Repeat to make a second row B.

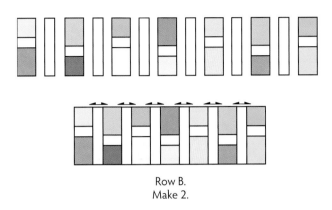

Row B.
Make 2.

3. Sew six of the white 3½" x 42" strips together end to end. From the pieced strip, cut three 66½"-long strips. Lay out the A and B rows and the white strips as shown. Sew the rows and strips together. Press the seam allowances toward the block rows.

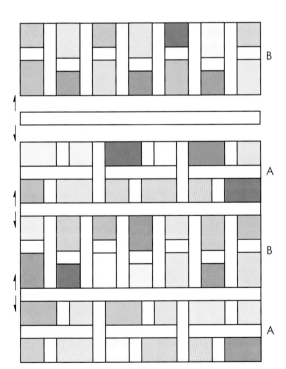

4. Sew the remaining white 3½" x 42" strips together end to end. Refer to "Borders" on page 75 to measure the length of the quilt top. From the pieced strip, cut two white strips to this length and sew them to the sides of the quilt top. Press the seam allowances toward the quilt center. Measure the width of the quilt top. From the remainder of the pieced strip, cut two white strips to this length and sew them to the top and bottom of the quilt top to complete the outer border. Press the seam allowances toward the borders.

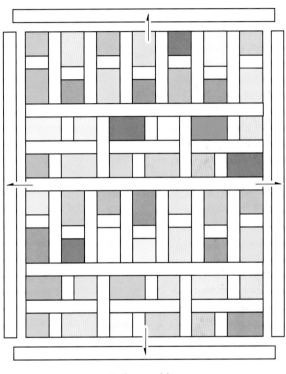

Quilt assembly

finishing the quilt

For detailed instructions on finishing techniques, refer to "Quiltmaking Basics" on pages 76–78. Use the 2¼"-wide strips to make and attach the binding.

pathways

Perfect for teens and grads, this quilt is sure to be cherished for years when made in school colors. I really love the playfulness of this quilt. The design feels improvised but is actually controlled, and makes a big statement.

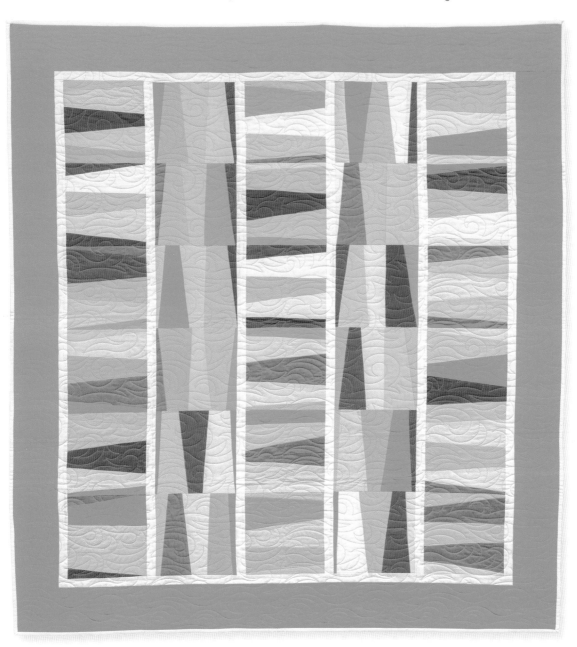

Finished quilt: 59" x 63½" • Finished block: 8½" x 8½ "

Designed by Rachel Griffith; pieced by KarrieLyne Winters; quilted by Darla Padilla.
Fabrics featured are Kona Cottons from Robert Kaufman Fabrics.

materials

Yardage is based on 42"-wide fabric unless otherwise specified.

12 fat quarters (18" x 21") of assorted solids for blocks

1⅛ yards of teal solid for outer border

1 yard of cream solid for sashing, inner border, and binding

3¾ yards of fabric for backing

63" x 68" piece of batting

cutting

From *each* fat quarter, cut:
- 2 strips, 11" x 18" (24 total)

From the cream solid, cut:
- 11 strips, 1½" x 42"
- 7 strips, 2¼" x 42"

From the teal solid, cut:
- 6 strips, 5½" x 42"

making the wedge blocks

1. Using your rotary cutter and ruler, make six cuts on each 11" x 18" strip to yield seven wedges per strip (168 total). You don't need to measure; the wedges should be wonky in appearance but have straight edges. Aim to make the wedges about the same size. This will make the blocks appear more balanced once the wedges are sewn together.

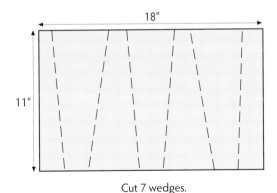

Cut 7 wedges.

2. Randomly join five different-color wedges to make a block. Press the seam allowances to one side. The block will be oversized. Use a square

ruler to trim the block to measure 9" x 9". Repeat to make a total of 30 blocks.

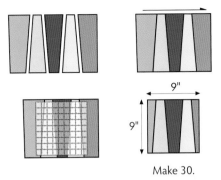

Make 30.

joining the wedges

When making the blocks, switching the narrow and wide ends of the wedges will make the blocks appear balanced. If the first wedge has a narrow end at the top, position the second wedge with the wide end at the top.

making the rows

This quilt is assembled in vertical rows with the blocks rotated 90° in two of the rows.

1. With the wedges positioned *horizontally,* lay out six blocks as shown. Join the blocks to make a row. Press the seam allowances in one direction. The row should measure 51½" long. Repeat to make a total of three of row A.

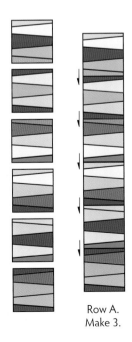

Row A.
Make 3.

2. With the wedges positioned *vertically*, lay out six blocks as shown. Join the blocks to make a row. Press the seam allowances in one direction. The row should measure 51½" long. Repeat to make a second row B.

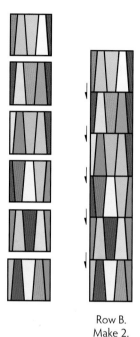

Row B.
Make 2.

assembling the quilt top

1. Sew the cream 1½"-wide strips together end to end. From the pieced strip, cut four 51½"-long strips. Lay out the A and B rows and the cream strips as shown. Sew the rows and strips together. Press the seam allowances toward the sashing strips.

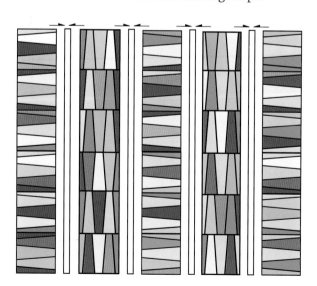

2. Refer to "Borders" on page 75 to measure the length of the quilt top. From the pieced cream strip, cut two strips to this length and sew them to the sides of the quilt top. Press the seam allowances toward the cream strips. Measure the width of the quilt top. From the remainder of the pieced strip, cut two cream strips to this length and sew them to the top and bottom of the quilt top to complete the inner border. Press the seam allowances toward the cream strips.

3. Sew the teal 5½"-wide strips end to end. Repeat step 2 to measure and cut the strips; then sew them to the quilt top for the outer border. Press all seam allowances toward the outer borders.

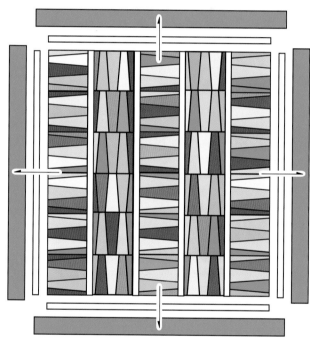

Quilt assembly

finishing the quilt

For detailed instructions on finishing techniques, refer to "Quiltmaking Basics" on pages 76–78. Use the 2¼"-wide strips to make and attach the binding.

it takes two

Two people falling in love and deciding to spend the rest of their lives together is a beautiful thing. I like this quilt's simplistic design and its ability to playfully grab your attention.

Finished quilt: 60½" x 60½" • Finished block: 12" x 12"
Designed by Rachel Griffith; pieced by Lani Padilla; quilted by Darla Padilla.
Fabrics featured are Pure Elements by Art Gallery Fabrics.

materials

Yardage is based on 42"-wide fabric unless otherwise specified.

16 fat quarters (18" x 21") of assorted dark solids for blocks

1⅜ yards of white solid for blocks and inner border

1⅛ yards of aqua solid for outer border

⅝ yard of fabric for binding

3¾ yards of fabric for backing

65" x 65" piece of batting

cutting

From *each* of the assorted dark solids, cut:
⊛ 1 square, 4¼" x 4¼"; cut in half diagonally to yield 2 triangles (32 total)
⊛ 2 strips, 1¼" x 6¼" (32 total)
⊛ 2 strips, 1¼" x 6¾" (32 total)
⊛ 2 strips, 1¼" x 8½" (32 total)
⊛ 2 strips, 2½" x 8½" (32 total)
⊛ 2 strips, 2½" x 12½" (32 total)

From the white solid, cut:
⊛ 2 strips, 4¼" x 42"; crosscut into 16 squares, 4¼" x 4¼". Cut the squares in half diagonally to yield 32 triangles
⊛ 20 strips, 1¼" x 42"; crosscut into:
   32 strips, 1¼" x 6¼"
   32 strips, 1¼" x 6¾"
   32 strips, 1¼" x 8½"
⊛ 5 strips, 1½" x 42"

From the aqua solid, cut:
⊛ 6 strips, 5½" x 42"

From the binding fabric, cut:
⊛ 7 strips, 2¼" x 42"

making the triangle units

1. Sew a dark 1¼" x 8½" strip to the long side of a white triangle. Press the seam allowances toward the dark strip. Trim the ends of the dark strip even with the short sides of the white triangle.

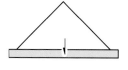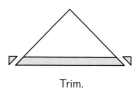

Trim.

2. Sew a matching dark 1¼" x 6¼" strip to one short side of the white triangle. Press the seam allowances toward the dark strip. Trim the end of the strip even with the strip along the bottom edge.

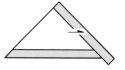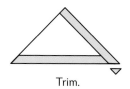

Trim.

3. Sew a matching dark 1¼" x 6¾" strip to the remaining side of the triangle as shown. Press the seam allowances toward the dark strip. Trim the end of the strip even with the strip along the bottom edge. Repeat the process to make a total of 32 triangle units with a white center.

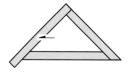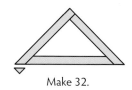

Make 32.

4. Repeat steps 1–3 to make 32 triangle units with a dark center and white strips.

Make 32.

making the triangle blocks

1. Lay out two matching triangles with white centers and two matching triangles with dark centers as shown. Join the triangles into pairs and press the seam allowances toward the dark strips. Join the triangle pairs to make a center unit. Press the seam allowances to one side. Trim the unit to measure 8½" x 8½". Make 16.

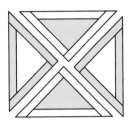 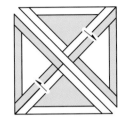

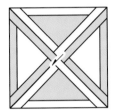

Make 16.

2. Select two matching 2½" x 8½" and two matching 2½" x 12½" strips that contrast with the block center. Sew the 8½" strips to the sides and the 12½" strips to the top and bottom. Press the seam allowances toward the just-added strips. Repeat to make a total of 16 blocks.

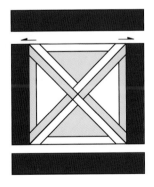 

Make 16.

assembling the quilt top

1. Lay out the blocks in four rows of four blocks each, rotating the blocks as shown. Sew the blocks together in rows. Press the seam allowances in opposite directions from row to row. Sew the rows together and press the seam allowances in one direction.

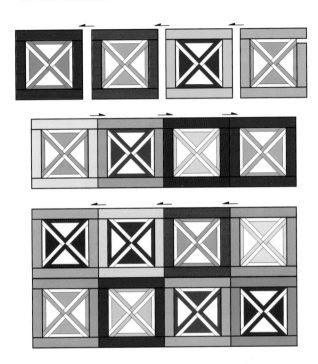

2. Sew the white 1½" x 42" strips together end to end. Refer to "Borders" on page 75 to measure the length of the quilt top. From the pieced strip, cut two white strips to this length and sew them to the sides of the quilt top. Press the seam allowances toward the inner border. Measure the width of the quilt top. From the remainder of the pieced strip, cut two white strips to this length and sew them to the top and bottom of the quilt top to complete the inner border. Press the seam allowances toward the inner border.

3. Sew the aqua 5½"-wide strips together end to end. Repeat step 2 to measure, and cut the strips; then sew them to the quilt top for the outer border. Press all seam allowances toward the outer borders.

finishing the quilt

For detailed instructions on finishing techniques, refer to "Quiltmaking Basics" on pages 76–78. Use the 2¼"-wide strips to make and attach the binding.

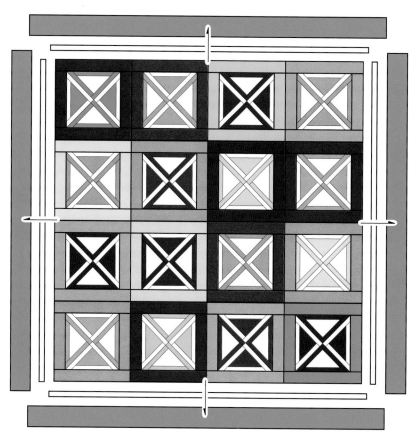

Quilt assembly

unconditional

Give the bride and groom a keepsake that can be used for many years. You can easily personalize this quilt by matching fabric to the wedding invitation.

Finished quilt: 72½" x 72½" • Finished block: 12" x 12"

Designed by Rachel Griffith; pieced by Molly Culley; quilted by Darla Padilla.
Fabrics featured are Bespoken and Paradise by Pat Bravo for Art Gallery Fabrics.

materials

Yardage is based on 42"-wide fabric unless otherwise specified.

4⅜ yards of cream solid for blocks, sashing, and border

13 fat eighths (9" x 21") of assorted prints for blocks

⅝ yard of fabric for binding

4⅝ yards of fabric for backing

77" x 77" piece of batting

cutting

From *each* of the assorted prints, cut:

⊕ 10 squares, 3⅞" x 3⅞" (130 total; 2 are extra)

From the cream solid, cut:

⊕ 13 strips, 3⅞" x 42"; crosscut into 128 squares, 3⅞" x 3⅞"

⊕ 6 strips, 3½" x 42"; crosscut into:
  4 strips, 3½" x 27½"
  8 strips, 3½" x 12½"

⊕ 2 strips, 6½" x 27½"

⊕ 9 strips, 6½" x 42"

From the binding fabric, cut:

⊕ 8 strips, 2¼" x 42"

making the arrow blocks

1. Referring to "Making Half-Square-Triangle Units" on page 74, pair a print 3⅞" square with each cream square to make 256 half-square-triangle units. Press the seam allowances toward the print triangles. The units should measure 3½" x 3½".

Make 256.

2. Lay out 16 half-square-triangle units in four rows of four units each as shown. Join the units in each row and press the seam allowances in opposite directions from row to row. Join the rows to complete the block. Press the seam allowances in one direction. Repeat to make a total of 16 Arrow blocks.

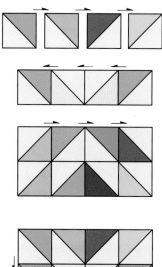
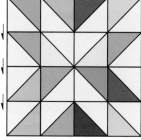

Make 16.

assembling the quilt top

1. Sew two Arrow blocks and one cream 3½" x 12½" strip together to make a row. Press the seam allowances toward the cream strip. Make a second block row. Then join the rows and a cream 3½" x 27½" strip as shown to complete a large block unit. Make four of these units.

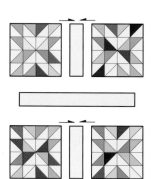
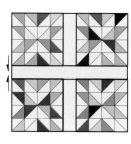

Make 4.

2. Sew two of the cream 6½" x 42" strips together end to end. From the pieced strip, cut one 60½"-long strip. Lay out the block units from step 1, the two cream 6½" x 27½" strips, and the cream 6½" x 60½" strip as shown. Join the blocks and cream 27½"-long strips into rows. Press the seam allowances toward the cream strips. Then join the rows and cream 60½"-long strip to complete the quilt-top center. Press the seam allowances toward the cream strip.

3. Sew the remaining cream 6½"-wide strips together end to end. Refer to "Borders" on page 75 to measure the length of the quilt top. From the pieced strip, cut two cream strips to this length and sew them to the sides of the quilt top. Press the seam allowances toward the outer border. Measure the width of the quilt top. From the remainder of the pieced strip, cut two cream strips to this length and sew them to the top and bottom of the quilt top to complete the outer border. Press the seam allowances toward the outer border.

finishing the quilt

For detailed instructions on finishing techniques, refer to "Quiltmaking Basics" on pages 76–78. Use the 2¼"-wide strips to make and attach the binding.

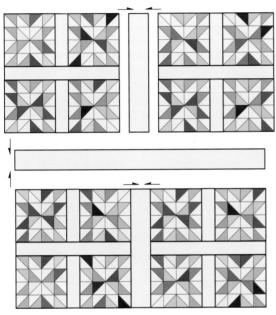

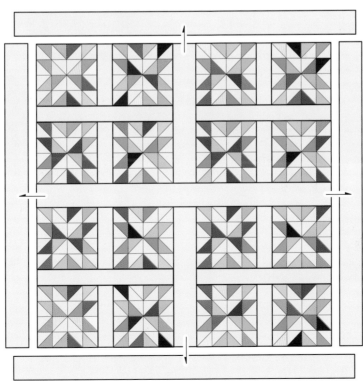

Quilt assembly

no place like home

A new house always needs a special touch, and nothing beats a homemade housewarming gift. I love that this quilt is full of color and can easily be used in any room of the house.

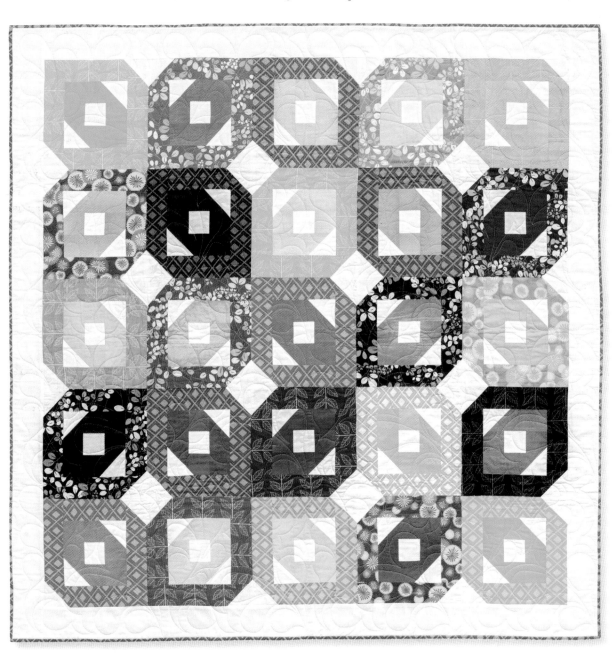

Finished quilt: 56½" x 56½" • Finished block: 10" x 10"

Designed by Rachel Griffith; pieced by Julie Herman; quilted by Darla Padilla.
Fabrics featured are Simply Color by V and Co. for Moda Fabrics.

materials

Yardage is based on 42"-wide fabric unless otherwise specified.

1⅝ yards of white solid for blocks and border

4 strips, 2½" x 42", *each* of purple, pink, and green prints for blocks

3 strips, 2½" x 42", *each* of aqua, orange, and gray prints for blocks

2 strips, 2½" x 42", *each* of yellow and navy prints for blocks

2 strips, 2½" x 42", *each* of purple, pink, green, aqua, orange, and gray solids for blocks

1 strip, 2½" x 42", *each* of yellow and navy solids for blocks

½ yard of fabric for binding

3⅝ yards of fabric for backing

61" x 61" piece of batting

cutting

From *each* of the print strips, cut:
- 2 rectangles, 2½" x 6½" (50 total)
- 2 rectangles, 2½" x 10½" (50 total)

From *each* of the navy, yellow, purple, pink, and green solid strips, cut:
- 4 squares, 2½" x 2½" (32 total)
- 4 rectangles, 2½" x 6½" (32 total)

From *each* of the aqua, orange, and gray solid strips, cut:
- 3 squares, 2½" x 2½" (6 of each color; 18 total)
- 3 rectangles, 2½" x 6½" (6 of each color; 18 total)

From the white solid, cut:
- 2 strips, 2½" x 42"; crosscut into 25 squares, 2½" x 2½"
- 8 strips, 3" x 42"; crosscut into 100 squares, 3" x 3"
- 6 strips, 3½" x 42"

From the binding fabric, cut:
- 6 strips, 2¼" x 42"

making the pineapple blocks

1. Lay out two solid-colored squares, two solid-colored rectangles (all matching), and one white 2½" square as shown. Join the squares and press the seam allowances away from the white square. Then join the three rectangles to make a center unit. Press the seam allowances toward the solid rectangles. Make 25 units.

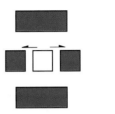

Make 25.

2. Draw a line from corner to corner on the wrong side of each white 3" square. With right sides together, place a marked square on opposite corners of a center unit as shown. Sew on the marked line. Repeat to sew marked squares to the remaining center units. Set aside the remaining marked squares for step 5.

Make 25.

3. Trim away the corner fabric, leaving a ¼"-wide seam allowance. Press the seam allowances toward the resulting triangle. Make 25 units.

Make 25.

4. Using print rectangles from the same color family as the center unit, sew 2½" x 6½" rectangles to opposite sides of the unit from step 3. Then sew a matching 2½" x 10½" rectangle to the top and bottom to complete the unit. Press all seam allowances toward the just-added rectangles. Make 25.

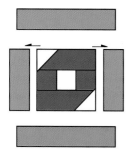 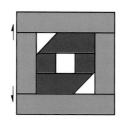

Make 25.

5. Place a marked square from step 3 on opposite corners of a center unit as shown. Sew on the marked line. Repeat to sew marked squares to the remaining units.

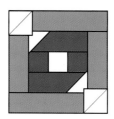

6. Trim the excess corner fabric, leaving a ¼"-wide seam allowance to complete the block. Press the seam allowances toward the resulting triangle. Trim and square up the block to measure 10½" x 10½". Make 25 Pineapple blocks.

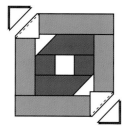 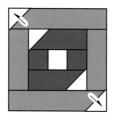

Make 25.

assembling the quilt top

1. Lay out the Pineapple blocks in five rows of five blocks each, rotating the blocks as shown below. Sew the blocks together into rows. Press the seam allowances in opposite directions from row to row.

2. Sew the rows together and press the seam allowances in one direction.

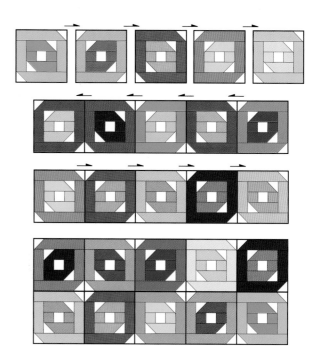

3. Sew the white 3½" x 42" strips together end to end. Refer to "Borders" on page 75 to measure the length of the quilt top. From the pieced strip, cut two white strips to this length and sew them to the sides of the quilt top. Press the seam allowances toward the outer border. Measure the width

of the quilt top. From the remainder of the pieced strip, cut two white strips to this length and sew them to the top and bottom of the quilt top to complete the outer border. Press the seam allowances toward the outer border.

finishing the quilt

For detailed instructions on finishing techniques, refer to "Quiltmaking Basics" on pages 76–78. Use the 2¼"-wide strips to make and attach the binding.

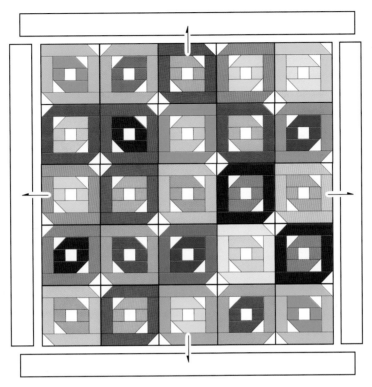

Quilt assembly

happily ever after

Hearing about couples who have remained married for years upon years makes my heart happy. I look up to these relationship superstars. This quilt is a celebration of time spent together.

Finished quilt: 54½" x 54½" • Finished block: 9" x 9"

Designed and pieced by Rachel Griffith; quilted by Darla Padilla.
Fabrics featured are Palladium and Maasai Mara by Dear Stella Fabrics.

materials

Yardage is based on 42"-wide fabric unless otherwise specified.

9 fat quarters (18" x 21") of assorted light-gray prints for sashing

1⅛ yards of gray solid for blocks

4 fat quarters of assorted dark-gray prints for sashing

3 fat quarters of assorted yellow prints for blocks

½ yard of fabric for binding

3½ yards of fabric for backing

59" x 59" piece of batting

cutting

From the gray solid, cut:

⊛ 18 strips, 2" x 42"; crosscut into:

    32 strips, 2" x 6½"

    48 strips, 2" x 9½"

    4 squares, 2" x 2"

From the assorted yellow prints, cut *a total of:*

⊛ 16 squares, 6½" x 6½"

From the assorted dark-gray prints, cut *a total of:*

⊛ 200 squares, 2" x 2"

⊛ 25 squares, 3½" x 3½"

From the assorted light-gray prints, cut *a total of:*

⊛ 40 rectangles, 3½" x 9½"

⊛ 20 rectangles, 2" x 3½"

From the binding fabric, cut:

⊛ 6 strips, 2¼" x 42"

making the square blocks

Sew gray 2" x 6½" strips to opposite sides of a yellow square. Press the seam allowances toward the gray strips. Sew gray 2" x 9½" strips to the top and bottom of the unit to complete the block. Press the seam allowances toward the gray strips. Repeat to make a total of 16 blocks.

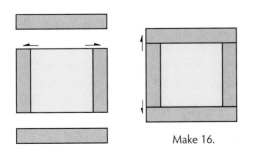

Make 16.

making the sashing

1. Draw a line from corner to corner on the wrong side of each dark-gray 2" square. Place a marked square on one end of a light-gray 2" x 3½" rectangle, right sides together, and sew on the line as shown. Trim away the corner fabric, leaving a ¼"-wide seam allowance. Press the seam allowances toward the resulting triangle.

2. Place a second marked square on the opposite end of the rectangle, right sides together. Sew on the marked line and trim as before. Press the seam allowances toward the resulting triangle. Repeat the process to make a total of 20 flying-geese units.

Make 20.

3. Place a marked dark-gray square from step 1 on two corners of a light-gray 3½" x 9½" rectangle, right sides together, and sew on the marked lines as shown. Trim away the corner fabric, leaving a ¼"-wide seam allowance. Press the seam allowances toward the resulting triangles.

4. Place marked squares on the remaining two corners of the rectangle, right sides together. Sew on the marked lines and trim as before. Press the seam allowances toward the resulting triangles. Repeat the process to make a total of 40 sashing units.

Make 40.

assembling the quilt top

1. Lay out five flying-geese units, four gray 2" x 9½" strips, and two gray 2" squares as shown. Join the pieces to make the top row and press the seam allowances toward the gray strips and squares. Repeat to make the bottom row.

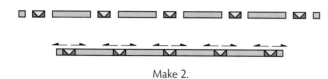

Make 2.

2. Lay out five dark-gray 3½" squares, four sashing units, and two flying-geese units as shown. Join the pieces to make a sashing row and press the seam allowances toward the dark-gray squares. Repeat to make a total of five rows.

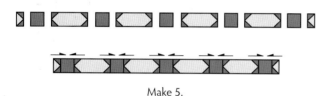

Make 5.

3. Lay out five sashing units, four blocks, and two gray 2" x 9½" strips as shown. Join the pieces to make a block row and press the seam allowances toward the blocks and gray strips. Repeat to make a total of four rows.

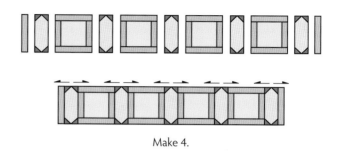

Make 4.

4. Lay out the rows as shown in the quilt assembly diagram below. Sew the rows together to complete the quilt top. Press the seam allowances toward the sashing rows.

finishing the quilt

For detailed instructions on finishing techniques, refer to "Quiltmaking Basics" on pages 76–78. Use the 2¼"-wide strips to make and attach the binding.

Quilt assembly

around the block

Retirement definitely deserves to be recognized as a lifetime achievement. I love the design play of this quilt. It's simple yet effective, and perfect for gift giving.

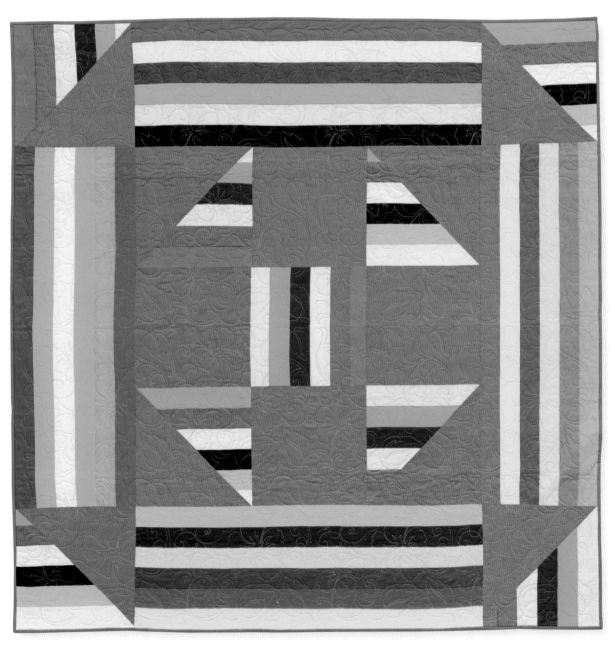

Finished quilt: 60½" x 60½" • Finished center block: 36" x 36"
Designed by Rachel Griffith; pieced by Molly Culley; quilted by Darla Padilla.
Fabrics featured are Kona Cottons by Robert Kaufman Fabrics.

materials

Yardage is based on 42"-wide fabric unless otherwise specified.

36 strips, 2½" x 42", of assorted solids for center block and border

1¼ yards of gray solid for center block and border

⅝ yard of fabric for binding

3¾ yards of fabric for backing

65" x 65" piece of batting

cutting

From the gray solid, cut:

❀ 3 strips, 12½" x 42"; crosscut into:
  4 squares, 12½" x 12½"
  4 rectangles, 12½" x 13¼"

From the binding fabric, cut:

❀ 7 strips, 2¼" x 42"

making the strip blocks

1. Referring to "Sewing Strips" on page 75, join six different solid 2½" x 42" strips to make a strip set. Press the seam allowances in one direction. Repeat to make a total of six strip sets. They should measure 12½" wide.

Make 6 strip sets.

2. From one strip set, cut one 12½" square and two 12½" x 13¼" rectangles. From another strip set, cut two 12½" x 13¼" rectangles. From the remaining strip sets, cut four 12½" x 36½" rectangles.

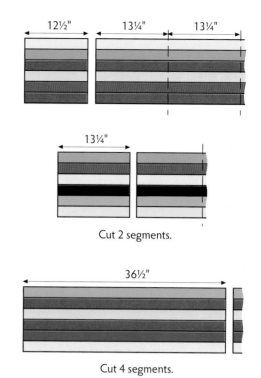

Cut 2 segments.

Cut 4 segments.

making the pieced squares

1. On the wrong side of each gray 12½" x 13¼" rectangle, make a mark along the edge of the fabric, ⅜" from the bottom-left corner as shown. Make a second mark ⅜" from the top-right corner. Draw a diagonal line connecting the marks. Place the marked rectangle right sides together with a 12½" x 13¼" strip-set segment, making sure the segment is oriented as shown. Sew ¼" from each side of the marked line.

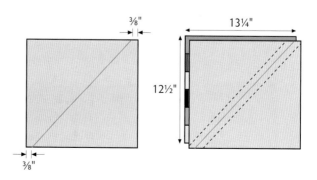

2. Cut the rectangles apart on the marked line and press the seam allowances toward the gray triangles to make two pieced squares. The squares should measure 12½" x 12½".

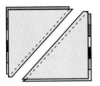

Make 2.

3. Repeat steps 1 and 2 using the remaining gray rectangles and 12½" x 13¼" strip-set segments, making sure to orient the segments as shown. Make six of these pieced squares.

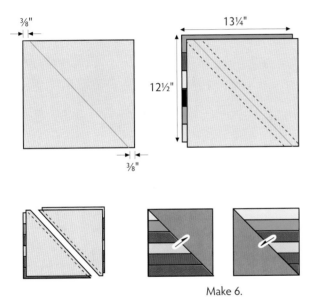

Make 6.

assembling the quilt top

1. Lay out four pieced squares, the 12½" strip-set square, and the gray 12½" squares in three rows, making sure to orient the pieced squares as shown above right. Join the squares into rows and press the seam allowances toward the

gray squares. Join the rows to complete the center block. Press the seam allowances toward the center.

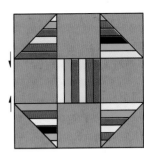

2. Sew 12½" x 36½" strip-set rectangles to opposite sides of the center block. Press the seam allowances away from the center block. Sew pieced squares to the ends of the two remaining 36½"-long strip-set rectangles and press the seam allowances toward the segments. Sew these strips to the top and bottom of the quilt top. Press the seam allowances toward the just-added strips.

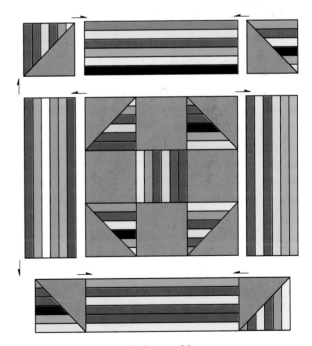

Quilt assembly

finishing the quilt

For detailed instructions on finishing techniques, refer to "Quiltmaking Basics" on pages 76–78. Use the 2¼"-wide strips to make and attach the binding.

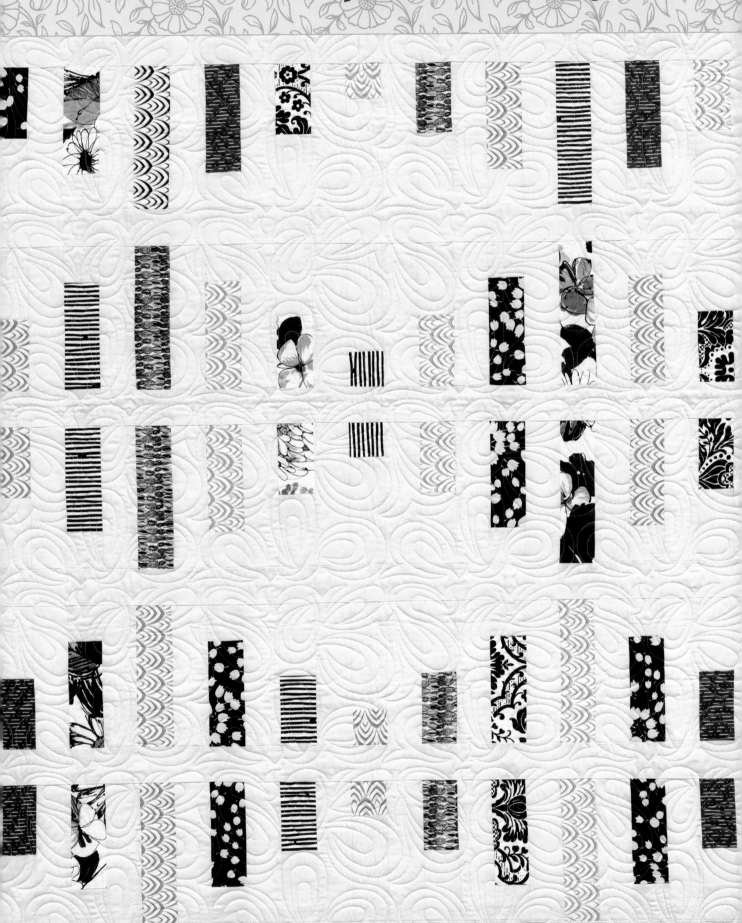

farsighted

Everyone gets a little homesick, but wrapping up in a quilt can be so comforting. I love pairing busy fabrics with a simple design. This quilt would make any college student feel right at home.

Finished quilt: 60½" x 60½"

Designed and pieced by Rachel Griffith; quilted by Darla Padilla.
Fabrics featured are Terrain and Cuzco by Kate Spain for Moda Fabrics

materials

Yardage is based on 42"-wide fabric unless otherwise specified.

8 fat quarters (18" x 21") of assorted light-colored prints

8 fat quarters of assorted dark-colored prints

⅝ yard of fabric for binding

3⅞ yards of fabric for backing

65" x 65" piece of batting

cutting

From the assorted light-colored prints, cut *a total of*:

⊕ 4 squares, 15½" x 15½"

⊕ 4 squares, 15⅞" x 15⅞"

From the assorted dark-colored prints, cut *a total of*:

⊕ 4 squares, 15½" x 15½"

⊕ 4 squares, 15⅞" x 15⅞"

From the binding fabric, cut:

⊕ 7 strips, 2¼" x 42"

assembling the quilt top

1. Referring to "Making Half-Square-Triangle Units" on page 74, pair each light 15⅞" square with a dark 15⅞" squares to make eight half-square-triangle units. Press the seam allowances toward the dark triangle. The units should measure 15½" x 15½".

15½"

15½"

Make 8.

2. Lay out the half-square-triangle units and assorted 15½" squares in four rows, alternating the units and squares as shown. Sew the pieces together into rows as shown, above right. Press the seam allowances in opposite directions from row to row.

3. Sew the rows together. Press the seam allowances in one direction.

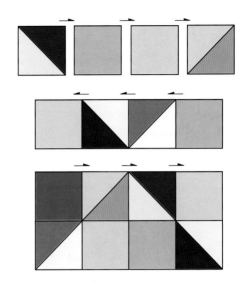

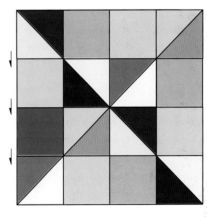

Quilt assembly

finishing the quilt

For detailed instructions on finishing techniques, refer to "Quiltmaking Basics" on pages 76–78. Use the 2¼"-wide strips to make and attach the binding.

look to the stars

Although it's honorable, deployment can take its toll on both soldiers and their families. My husband has a military background, so we've seen our fair share of deployments, and trust me, gestures like this quilt, given to the soldier or the soldier's family, can make someone's week.

Finished quilt: 66" x 66" • Finished block: 12" x 12"

Designed and pieced by Rachel Griffith; quilted by Darla Padilla.
Fabrics featured are Heirloom and Lanikai by Dear Stella Fabrics.

materials

Yardage is based on 42"-wide fabric unless otherwise specified.

3½ yards of white solid for blocks and borders

18 fat eighths (9" x 21") of assorted blue and gray prints for blocks and borders

⅝ yard of fabric for binding

4¼ yards of fabric for backing

71" x 71" piece of batting

cutting

From the assorted blue and gray prints, cut a total of:

⊛ 96 squares, 3⅞" x 3⅞"

⊛ 20 squares, 3½" x 3½"

From the white solid, cut:

⊛ 9 strips, 3⅞" x 42"; crosscut into 96 squares, 3⅞" x 3⅞"

⊛ 5 strips, 3½" x 42"; crosscut into:
    2 strips, 3½" x 18½"
    2 strips, 3½" x 12½"
    8 squares, 3½" x 3½"

⊛ 1 strip, 6½" x 42"; crosscut into 5 squares, 6½" x 6½"

⊛ 2 strips, 6½" x 24½"

⊛ 2 strips, 6½" x 36½"

⊛ 4 strips, 9½" x 36½"

From the binding fabric, cut:

⊛ 7 strips, 2¼" x 42"

making the star blocks

1. Referring to "Making Half-Square-Triangle Units" on page 74, pair each assorted square with a white 3⅞" square to make 192 half-square-triangle units. The units should measure 3½" x 3½".

Make 192.

2. Lay out eight half-square-triangle units, four assorted blue and gray 3½" squares, and one white 6½" square as shown. Sew the pieces together into rows. Press the seam allowances in the direction indicated by the arrows. Join the rows and press the seam allowances toward the center. The block should measure 12½" square. Repeat to make a total of five Star blocks.

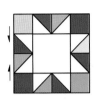 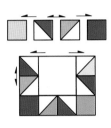

Make 5.

assembling the quilt top

1. Sew white 3½" x 12½" strips to opposite sides of a Star block. Press the seam allowances toward the white strips. Sew white 3½" x 18½" strips to the remaining two sides of the block. Press the seam allowances toward the just-added strips. Make one center block.

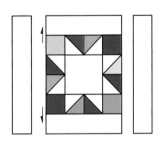 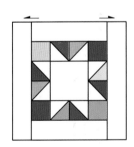

Make 1.

2. Lay out eight half-square-triangle units, one white 3½" square, and one Star block as shown on page 50. Join the pieces to make two rows. Join the rows to a Star block to make a corner block

as shown. Press the seam allowances toward the Star block. Make two of each block, making sure to orient the half-square-triangle units as shown.

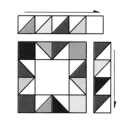

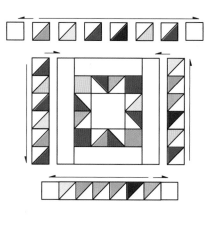

Make 2 of each.

3. Lay out 24 half-square-triangle units, four white 3½" squares, and the center block from step 1, making sure to orient the half-square-triangle units as shown. Sew the pieces together into rows. Press the seam allowances as indicated. Join the rows and press the seam allowances toward the center block.

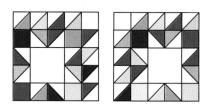

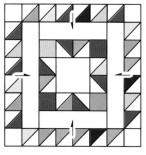

4. Sew white 6½" x 24½" strips to opposite sides of the unit from step 3. Press the seam allowances toward the white strips. Sew white 6½" x 36½" strips to the remaining two sides of the unit. Press the seam allowances toward the just-added strips.

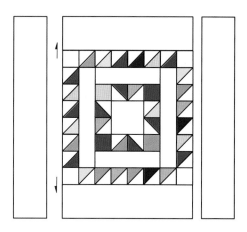

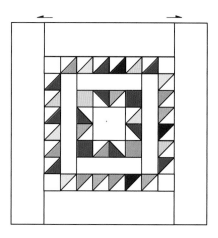

5. Lay out 24 half-square-triangle units and one white 9½" x 36½" strip, making sure to orient the half-square-triangle units as shown. Sew 12 half-square-triangle units together to make a row. Press the seam allowances in one direction. Make two rows and join the rows to opposite sides of

the white strip to make a border unit. Make two border units and two reversed border units.

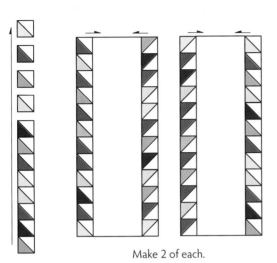

Make 2 of each.

6. Lay out the unit from step 4, the border units from step 5, and the corner blocks from step 2, making sure to orient the units and blocks as shown. Sew the units and blocks into rows. Press the seam allowances in the direction indicated. Join the rows to complete the quilt top. Press the seam allowances toward the center.

finishing the quilt

For detailed instructions on finishing techniques, refer to "Quiltmaking Basics" on pages 76–78. Use the 2¼"-wide strips to make and attach the binding.

Quilt assembly

second wind

When loved ones are facing an injury or illness, it's easy to feel powerless to help them. Presenting them with a quilt is a sure way to express your willingness to care and comfort.

Finished quilt: 65½" x 65½" • Finished block: 12" x 12"

Designed by Rachel Griffith; pieced by Lani Padilla; quilted by Darla Padilla.
Fabrics featured are Stitch by Betz White for Robert Kaufman Fabrics.

materials

Yardage is based on 42"-wide fabric unless otherwise specified.

42 squares, 10" x 10", of assorted prints for blocks

1¼ yards of teal print for outer border

1 yard of gray print for blocks, middle border, and binding

⅝ yard of white solid for sashing and inner border

⅜ yard of yellow print for blocks

⅜ yard of burgundy print for blocks

¼ yard of green print for blocks

4⅛ yards of fabric for backing

70" x 70" piece of batting

cutting

From *each of 8* assorted 10" squares, cut:

⊛ 1 square, 8½" x 8½" (8 total)

From *each* of the remaining assorted 10" squares, cut:

⊛ 4 strips, 2" x 6½" (136 total; 8 are extra)

From the yellow print, cut:

⊛ 4 strips, 2½" x 42"; crosscut into:
   6 strips, 2½" x 8½"
   6 strips, 2½" x 12½"

From the burgundy print, cut:

⊛ 4 strips, 2½" x 42"; crosscut into:
   6 strips, 2½" x 8½"
   6 strips, 2½" x 12½"

From the green print, cut:

⊛ 2 strips, 2½" x 42"; crosscut into:
   2 strips, 2½" x 8½"
   2 strips, 2½" x 12½"

From the gray print, cut:

⊛ 2 strips, 2½" x 42"; crosscut into:
   2 strips, 2½" x 8½"
   2 strips, 2½" x 12½"
⊛ 6 strips, 1½" x 42"
⊛ 7 strips, 2¼" x 42"

From the white solid, cut:

⊛ 12 strips, 1½" x 42"; crosscut *4 of the strips* into:
   12 strips, 1½" x 12½"

From the teal print, cut:

⊛ 7 strips, 5½" x 42"

making the rail fence blocks

1. Join four assorted 2" x 6½" strips side by side to make a 6½" square. Press the seam allowances in one direction. Repeat to make a total of 32 units.

Make 32.

2. Lay out four units, rotating the units as shown. Join the units into rows and press the seam allowances in opposite directions from row to row. Join the rows to complete the block. Press the seam allowances in one direction. The block should measure 12½" x 12½". Repeat to make a total of eight blocks.

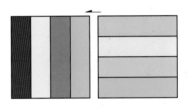

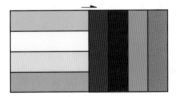

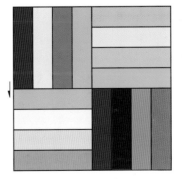

Make 8.

making the framed blocks

Sew matching burgundy, yellow, green, or gray 2½" x 8½" strips to opposite sides of a print 8½" square. Press the seam allowances toward the strips. Sew matching 2½" x 12½" strips to the top and bottom of the square to complete a block. Press the seam allowances toward the just-added strips. The block should measure 12½" x 12½". Repeat to make a total of eight blocks.

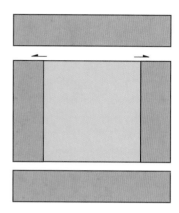

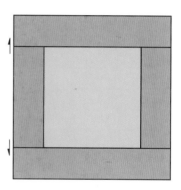

Make 8.

assembling the quilt top

1. Lay out two Rail Fence blocks, two Framed blocks, and three white 1½" x 12½" strips, alternating them as shown. Sew the blocks and strips together to make a row. Press the seam allowances toward the blocks. The row should measure 51½" long. Make a total of four rows.

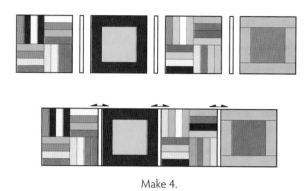

Make 4.

2. Sew four of the white 1½" x 42" strips together end to end. From the pieced strip, cut three 51½"-long sashing strips. Lay out the block rows from step 1 and the sashing strips, alternating them as shown. Sew the rows and strips together to complete the quilt center. Press the seam allowances towards the strips.

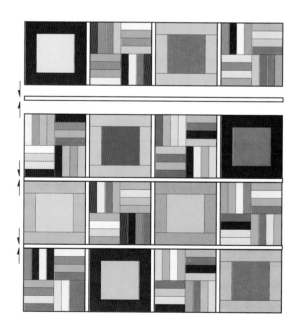

3. Sew the remaining white 1½" x 42" strips together end to end. Refer to "Borders" on page 75 to measure the length of the quilt top. From the pieced strip, cut two white strips to this length and sew them to the sides of the quilt top. Press the seam allowances toward the inner border. Measure the width of the quilt top. From the remainder of the pieced strip, cut two white strips to this length and sew them to the top and bottom of the quilt top to complete the inner border. Press the seam allowances toward the inner border.

4. Sew the gray 1½"-wide strips end to end. Repeat step 3 to measure and cut the strips; then sew them to the quilt top for the middle border. Press all seam allowances toward the middle borders.

5. Sew the teal 5½"-wide strips end to end. In the same manner as before, sew the strips to the quilt top for the outer border. Press.

finishing the quilt

For detailed instructions on finishing techniques, refer to "Quiltmaking Basics" on pages 76–78. Use the gray 2¼"-wide strips to make and attach the binding.

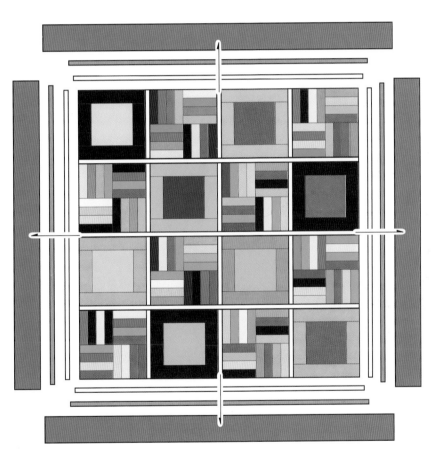

Quilt assembly

epilogue

For anyone struggling with addiction, depression, or a disorder, small gestures—like this quilt—can mean a lot.

Finished quilt: 55½" x 55½" • Finished block: 15" x 15"

Designed by Rachel Griffith; pieced by Jennifer Blosser; quilted by Darla Padilla.
Fabrics featured are Hyperreal Garden and Oval Elements by Art Gallery Fabrics.

materials

Yardage is based on 42"-wide fabric unless otherwise specified.

38 strips, 1½" x 42" of assorted prints for blocks
2 yards of white solid for blocks and border
½ yard of teal print for binding
3½ yards of fabric for backing
60" x 60" piece of batting

cutting

From the assorted strips, cut *each* strip in half to yield:

⊕ 76 strips, 1½" x 21" (1 is extra)

From the white solid, cut:

⊕ 2 strips, 15½" x 42"; crosscut into:
    9 strips, 3½" x 15½"
    18 strips, 2" x 15½"
⊕ 6 strips, 5½" x 42"

From the teal print, cut:

⊕ 6 strips, 2¼" x 42"

making the coin blocks

1. Referring to "Sewing Strips" on page 75, randomly sew 15 assorted strips together to make a strip set. Make five strip sets. Cut the strip sets into 18 segments, 5" wide.

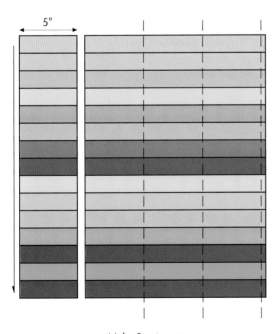

Make 5 strip sets.
Cut 18 segments.

2. Lay out two white 2" x 15½" strips, two strip-set segments, and one white 3½" x 15½" strip as shown. Join the strips and press the seam allowances toward the white strips. Repeat to make a total of nine Coin blocks.

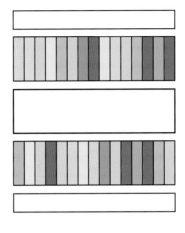

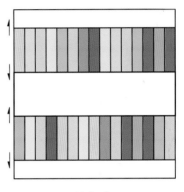

Make 9.

assembling the quilt top

1. Lay out the Coin blocks in three rows of three blocks each, rotating the blocks as shown in the quilt assembly diagram on page 58. Sew the blocks together in rows. Press the seam allowances in opposite directions from row to row.

Sew the rows together. Press the seam allowances toward the center.

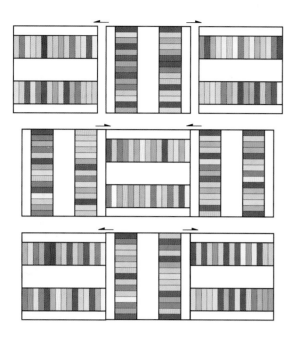

2. Sew the white 5½" x 42" strips together end to end. Refer to "Borders" on page 75 to measure the length of the quilt top. From the pieced strip, cut two white strips to this length and sew them to the sides of the quilt top. Press the seam allowances toward the outer border. Measure the width of the quilt top. From the remainder of the pieced strip, cut two white strips to this length and sew them to the top and bottom of the quilt top to complete the outer border. Press the seam allowances toward the outer border.

finishing the quilt

For detailed instructions on finishing techniques, refer to "Quiltmaking Basics" on pages 76–78. Use the 2¼"-wide strips to make and attach the binding.

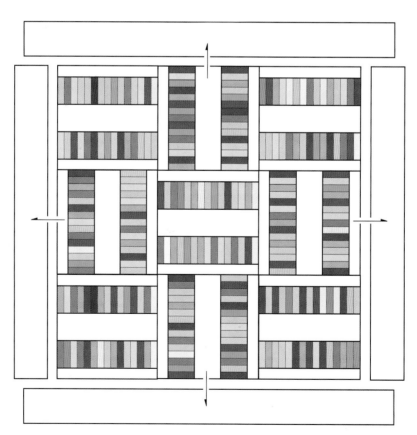

Quilt assembly

turnaround

*I believe that curling up with a pretty quilt is very therapeutic,
especially when everything else in the world seems out of place.*

Finished quilt: 58" x 58" • Finished block: 12" x 12"
*Designed by Rachel Griffith; pieced by Molly Culley; quilted by Darla Padilla.
Fabrics featured Kona Cottons by Robert Kaufman Fabrics.*

materials

Yardage is based on 42"-wide fabric unless otherwise specified.

7 strips, 2½" x 42", of assorted green solids for blocks

14 strips, 2½" x 42", of assorted pink solids for blocks

22 strips, 2½" x 42", of assorted aqua solids for blocks

1⅛ yards of gray solid for sashing and border

⅝ yard of dark-pink solid for sashing squares and binding

3¾ yards of fabric for backing

63" x 63" piece of batting

cutting

From the assorted green strips, cut:
- 16 rectangles, 2½" x 3½" (A)
- 16 rectangles, 2" x 2½" (B)
- 16 rectangles, 2½" x 5" (C)
- 16 rectangles, 2" x 4½" (D)

From the assorted pink strips, cut:
- 16 strips, 2½" x 6½" (E)
- 16 strips, 2" x 6½" (F)
- 16 strips, 2½" x 8" (G)
- 16 strips, 2" x 8½" (H)

From the assorted aqua strips, cut:
- 16 strips, 2½" x 9½" (I)
- 16 strips, 2" x 10½" (J)
- 16 strips, 2½" x 11" (K)
- 16 strips, 2" x 12½" (L)

From the gray solid, cut:
- 14 strips, 2½" x 42"; crosscut *8 of the strips* into 24 strips, 2½" x 12½"

From the dark-pink solid, cut:
- 9 squares, 2½" x 2½"
- 7 strips, 2¼" x 42"

making the quarter log cabin blocks

1. Sew a green A rectangle to a green B rectangle. Press the seam allowances toward B. Repeat to make 16 units.

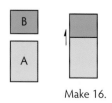

Make 16.

2. Sew a green C rectangle to each A/B unit to make 16 units. Press the seam allowances toward C. Repeat to make 16 units.

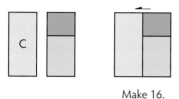

Make 16.

3. Sew a green D rectangle to each unit from step 2 to make 16 units. Press the seam allowances toward D. Repeat to make 16 units.

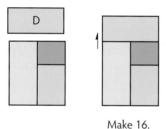

Make 16.

4. Sew a pink E strip to each unit from step 3 to make 16 units. Press the seam allowances toward E. Repeat to make 16 units.

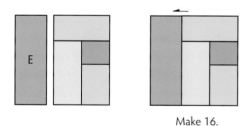

Make 16.

5. Referring to the cutting list, continue in the same manner as before, adding strips F–L in alphabetical order to each unit to complete the blocks. Press the seam allowances toward each newly added strip. Make a total of 16 blocks.

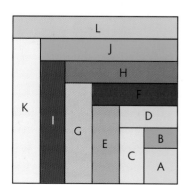

Make 16.

assembling the quilt top

1. Join three dark-pink 2½" squares and four gray 2½" x 12½" strips as shown to make a sashing row. Press the seam allowances toward the gray strips. Make a total of three sashing rows.

Make 3.

2. Lay out four blocks and three gray 2½" x 12½" strips, rotating the blocks as shown. Sew the blocks and strips together to make a block row. Press the seam allowances toward the gray strips. Make two of each row.

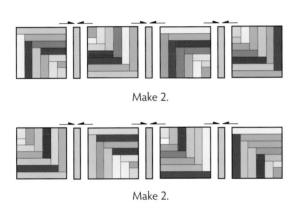

Make 2.

Make 2.

3. Sew the block rows and sashing rows together, alternating them as shown. Press the seam allowances towards the sashing rows.

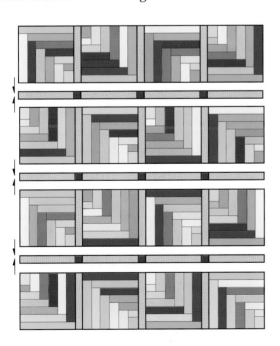

4. Sew the gray 2½" x 42" strips together end to end. Refer to "Borders" on page 75 to measure the length of the quilt top. From the pieced strip, cut two gray strips to this length and sew them to the sides of the quilt top. Press the seam allowances toward the outer border. Measure the width of the quilt top. From the remainder of the pieced strip, cut two gray strips to this length and sew them to the top and bottom of the quilt top to complete the outer border. Press the seam allowances toward the outer border.

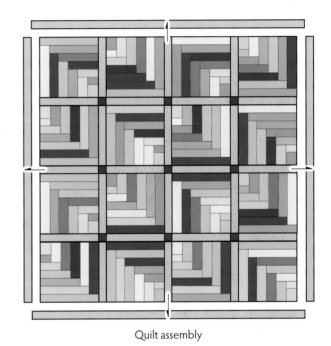

Quilt assembly

finishing the quilt

For detailed instructions on finishing techniques, refer to "Quiltmaking Basics" on pages 76–78. Use the dark-pink 2¼"-wide strips to make and attach the binding.

heartfelt

Nothing can replace a lost loved one, but wrapping someone in a quilt is a great way to make them feel comforted. This quilt can easily reflect a loved one's personality and tastes by your color choices—or even the use of old garments as scraps for the patchwork.

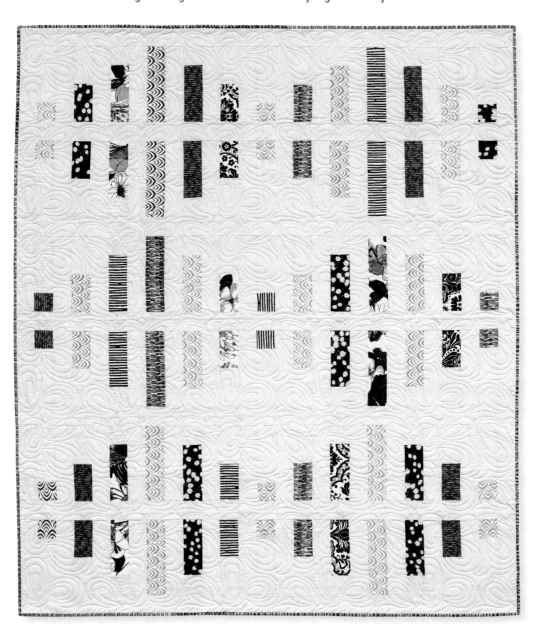

Finished quilt: 54½" x 62½" • Finished block: 8" x 54"

Designed by Rachel Griffith; pieced by Molly Culley; quilted by Darla Padilla.
Fabrics featured are Marea by Dear Stella Fabrics.

materials

Yardage is based on 42"-wide fabric unless otherwise specified.

6 fat quarters (18" x 21") of assorted prints for blocks
3 yards of cream solid for blocks and sashing
⅝ yard of fabric for binding
3½ yards of fabric for backing
59" x 67" piece of batting

cutting

From *each* of the assorted prints, cut:

❀ 4 strips, 2½" x 21"; crosscut into:
    4 squares, 2½" x 2½" (24 total; 6 are extra)
    4 strips, 2½" x 4½" (24 total)
    4 strips, 2½" x 6½" (24 total)
    2 strips, 2½" x 8½" (12 total)

From the cream solid, cut:

❀ 39 strips, 2½" x 42"; crosscut 29 of the strips into:
    84 strips, 2½" x 8½"
    18 strips, 2½" x 6½"
    24 strips, 2½" x 4½"
    24 squares, 2½" x 2½"

From the binding fabric, cut:

❀ 7 strips, 2¼" x 42"

making the wavelength rows

1. Join a print 2½" square to a cream 2½" x 6½" strip to make 18 units. Press the seam allowances toward the square.

Make 18.

2. Join each print 2½" x 4½" strip to one end of a cream 2½" x 4½" strip to make 24 units. Press the seam allowances toward the assorted strip.

Make 24.

3. Join each print 2½" x 6½" strip to a cream 2½" square to make 24 units. Press the seam allowances toward the assorted strip.

Make 24.

4. Lay out three units from step 1, four units from step 2, four units from step 3, two assorted print 2½" x 8½" strips, and 14 cream 2½" x 8½" strips as shown. Join the strips to complete a Wavelength row. Press the seam allowances toward the cream strips. The row should measure 8½" x 54½". Make a total of six rows, referring to the photo for placement guidance.

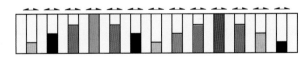

Make 6.

assembling the quilt top

1. Sew the remaining cream 2½" x 42" strips together end to end. From the pieced strip, cut seven cream 54½"-long sashing strips.
2. Lay out the Wavelength rows and the sashing strips in horizontal rows, rotating the Wavelength rows and alternating them with the sashing strips as shown below.
3. Sew the rows together to complete the quilt top. Press the seam allowances toward the sashing strips.

finishing the quilt

For detailed instructions on finishing techniques, refer to "Quiltmaking Basics" on pages 76–78. Use the 2¼"-wide strips to make and attach the binding.

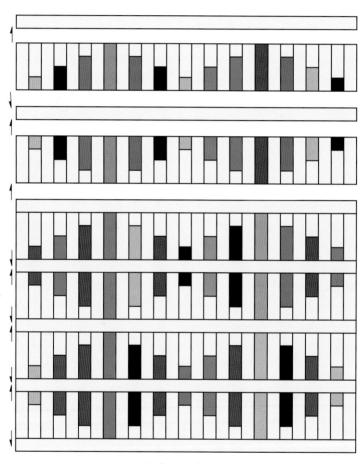

Quilt assembly

sincerely

Who doesn't love knowing that someone's thinking of them? Everyone deserves a "just because" present every now and then. What's better than a quilt?

Finished quilt: 69½" x 69½"
Designed and pieced by Rachel Griffith; quilted by Darla Padilla.
Fabrics featured are Pedal Pusher by Dear Stella Fabrics.

materials

Yardage is based on 42"-wide fabric unless otherwise specified.

16 fat quarters (18" x 21") of assorted prints for squares and rectangles

3 yards of gray solid for background and border

⅝ yard of fabric for binding

4½ yards of fabric for backing

74" x 74" piece of batting

cutting

From the assorted prints, cut *a total of:*
- 4 rectangles, 12½" x 15½"
- 6 squares, 9½" x 9½"
- 6 rectangles, 6½" x 9½"
- 4 squares, 6½" x 6½"

From the gray solid, cut:
- 9 strips, 3½" x 42"; crosscut *6 of the strips* into:
    - 1 strip, 3½" x 33½"
    - 2 strips, 3½" x 27½"
    - 2 strips, 3½" x 12½"
    - 8 rectangles, 3½" x 9½"
    - 4 rectangles, 3½" x 6½"
- 7 strips, 9½" x 42"

From the binding fabric, cut:
- 8 strips, 2¼" x 42" strips

assembling the quilt top

1. Lay out the four print 12½" x 15½" rectangles, the two gray 3½" x 12½" strips, and the gray 3½" x 33½" strip as shown. Join the rectangles and shorter gray strips into rows and press the seam allowances toward the gray strips. Then join the rows and longer gray strip to complete the center unit. Press the seam allowances toward the gray strip.

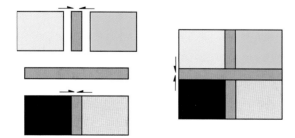

2. Lay out two print 6½" squares, one print 6½" x 9½" rectangle, and two gray 3½" x 6½" rectangles as shown. Join the pieces to make a border unit and press the seam allowances toward the gray strips. Repeat to make a second border unit.

3. Lay out the center unit from step 1, the border units from step 2, and the two gray 3½" x 27½" strips as shown. Join the pieces to make the center row. Press the seam allowances toward the gray strips. The center row should measure 51½" wide.

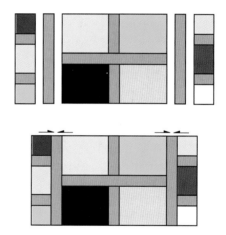

4. Lay out two print 6½" x 9½" rectangles, three print 9½" squares, and four gray 3½" x 9½" rectangles as shown. Join the pieces to make a border unit and press the seam allowances toward the gray strips. The border unit should measure 51½" long. Repeat to make a second border unit.

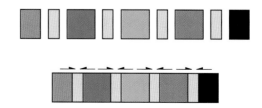

5. Join the three gray 3½" x 42" strips end to end. From the pieced strip, cut two 51½"-long strips. Lay out the center row from step 3, the border units from step 4, and the two gray strips as shown. Join the pieces to complete the quilt center. Press the seam allowances toward the gray strips.

6. Sew the gray 9½" x 42" strips together end to end. Refer to "Borders" on page 75 to measure the length of the quilt top. From the pieced strip, cut two gray strips to this length and sew them to the sides of the quilt top. Press the seam allowances toward the outer border. Measure the width of the quilt top. From the remainder of the pieced strip, cut two gray strips to this length and sew them to the top and bottom of the quilt top to complete the outer border. Press the seam allowances toward the outer border.

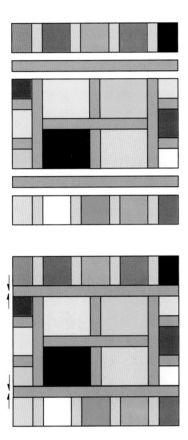

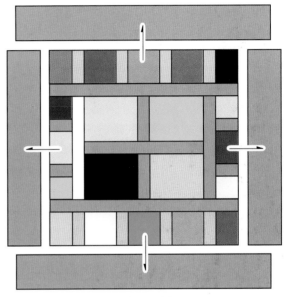

Quilt assembly

finishing the quilt

For detailed instructions on finishing techniques, refer to "Quiltmaking Basics" on pages 76–78. Use the 2¼"-wide strips to make and attach the binding.

embrace

Tragedy, in any capacity, takes a toll on everyone involved. Draping a quilt around someone's shoulder seems like a small gesture, but it can mean the world to someone in pain.

Finished quilt: 51½" x 51½" • Finished block: 9" x 9"

Designed by Rachel Griffith; pieced by Lani Padilla; quilted by Darla Padilla.
Fabrics featured are Bella Solids by Moda Fabrics.

materials

Yardage is based on 42"-wide fabric unless otherwise specified.

1½ yards of cream solid for blocks, sashing, and border

½ yard *each* of light-orange, peach, and dark-green solids for blocks

⅜ yard *each* of light-green and yellow solids for blocks

¼ yard *each* of brown and orange solids for blocks

½ yard of fabric for binding

3½ yards of fabric for backing

56" x 56" piece of batting

cutting

From the cream solid, cut:
- 26 strips, 1½" x 42"; crosscut *5 of the strips* into 20 strips, 1½" x 9½"
- 4 strips, 2" x 42"

From the light-orange solid, cut:
- 8 strips, 1½" x 42"

From the light-green solid, cut:
- 7 strips, 1½" x 42"

From the peach solid, cut:
- 4 strips, 1½" x 42"
- 3 strips, 2" x 42"

From the dark-green solid, cut:
- 3 strips, 1½" x 42"
- 4 strips, 2" x 42"

From the yellow solid, cut:
- 7 strips, 1½" x 42"

From the brown solid, cut:
- 3 strips, 1½" x 42"

From the orange solid, cut:
- 3 strips, 2" x 42"

From the binding fabric, cut:
- 6 strips, 2¼" x 42" strips

making the striped blocks

1. Referring to "Sewing Strips" on page 75, sew the following strips together in the order listed to make strip set A. Press the seam allowances in one direction. Make four of these strip sets.
   - Cream: 1½"-wide strip
   - Light orange: 1½"-wide strip
   - Light green: 1½"-wide strip
   - Cream: 2"-wide strip
   - Peach: 1½"-wide strip
   - Light orange: 1½"-wide strip
   - Dark green: 2"-wide strip
   - Yellow: 1½"-wide strip

2. Measure the width of the pressed strip sets; they should measure 9½". Cut each strip set into 9½"-wide segments to make 13 of block A.

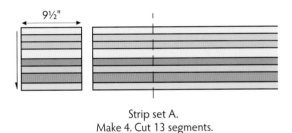

9½"

Strip set A.
Make 4. Cut 13 segments.

3. Sew the following strips together in the order listed to make strip set B. Press the seam allowances in one direction. Make three of these strip sets.
   - Cream: 1½"-wide strip
   - Yellow: 1½"-wide strip
   - Dark green: 1½"-wide strip
   - Peach: 2"-wide strip
   - Cream: 1½"-wide strip
   - Brown: 1½"-wide strip
   - Orange: 2"-wide strip
   - Light green: 1½"-wide strip

4. Measure the width of the pressed strip sets; they should measure 9½". Cut each strip set into 9½"-wide segments to make 12 of block B.

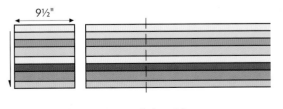

9½"

Strip set B.
Make 3. Cut 12 segments.

assembling the quilt top

1. Lay out three A blocks, two B blocks, and four cream 1½" x 9½" sashing strips, alternating and rotating the blocks as shown. Join the pieces to make a row. Press the seam allowances toward the sashing strips. Make three rows.

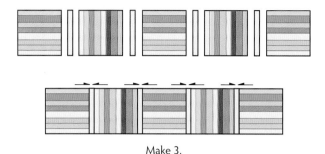

Make 3.

2. Lay out three B blocks, two A blocks, and four cream 1½" x 9½" sashing strips, alternating and rotating the blocks as shown. Join the pieces to make a row. Press the seam allowances toward the sashing strips. Make two rows.

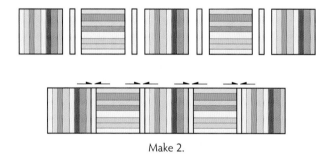

Make 2.

3. Sew five of the cream 1½" x 42" strips together end to end. From the pieced strip, cut four 49½"-long sashing strips. Lay out the rows from steps 1 and 2 with the sashing strips, alternating them as shown. Sew the rows and strips together to complete the quilt center. Press the seam allowances toward the strips.

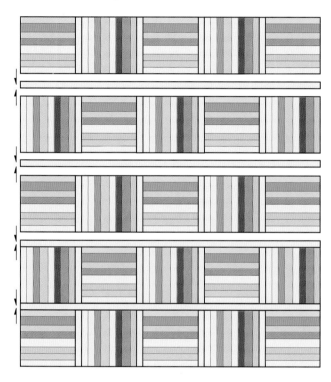

4. Sew the remaining cream 1½" x 42" strips together end to end. Refer to "Borders" on page 75 to measure the length of the quilt top. From the pieced strip, cut two cream strips to this length and sew them to the sides of the quilt top. Press the seam allowances toward the outer border. Measure the width of the quilt top. From the remainder of the pieced strip, cut two cream strips to this length and sew them to the top and bottom of the quilt top to complete the outer border. Press the seam allowances toward the outer border.

finishing the quilt

For detailed instructions on finishing techniques, refer to "Quiltmaking Basics" on pages 76–78. Use the 2¼"-wide strips to make and attach the binding.

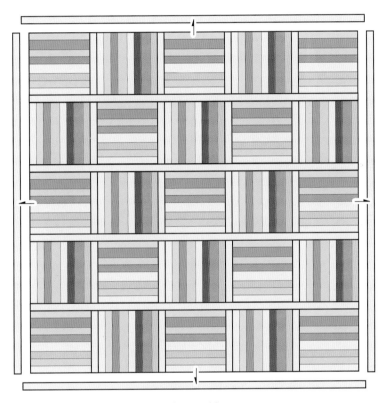

Quilt assembly

quiltmaking basics

The following pages include all the basic information you need to start and finish your quilt, from choosing fabrics to binding.

choosing fabric

Whether it's the color, design, or texture, fabric easily grabs our attention. Some quilters have enough fabric to be candidates for the television show "Hoarders," while others stock just enough fabric for the quilts on their quilting to-do list. The best fabric for making a quilt is 100% cotton because it minimizes seam distortion, presses crisply, and is easy to quilt. Unless otherwise noted, quantities in the materials lists are based on 42"-wide fabric. Please note extra yardage is factored in to allow for minor errors and shrinkage.

prewashing vs. not prewashing

You might want to sit down for this, but I never prewash my fabrics. Prewashing your fabrics is a choice, not an obligation. I know my great-grandmother would've had a fit if she heard me tell you that you don't have to prewash your fabrics, but let's face it—we're working with high-quality dyes and cottons nowadays. With that being said, I stand behind not prewashing fabrics purchased at quilt shops; however, you may want to prewash bargain-store fabrics. I know that some people are nervous about red colors running in the first wash of the quilt, and that's understandable, but you can use a dye-catcher sheet (check your local store's laundry aisle).

pressing

First things first, ironing and pressing are two different things. When you iron, you slide the iron back and forth with pressure to remove wrinkles and creases from your fabrics. When you press, you set the iron down on the desired area to set your seams. A lot of quilters tend to warp their piecing and their blocks due to ironing when they should

be pressing. Remember, iron your fabrics before cutting. Press your fabrics while constructing. Easy peasy. In quilting, almost every seam should be pressed before the piece is sewn to another. Instructions in this book generally tell you which direction to press the seam allowances. When in doubt, press the seam allowances toward the darker fabric. When joining rows of blocks, alternate the direction the seam allowances are pressed to create opposing seam allowances. This will ensure flat corners and matching intersections.

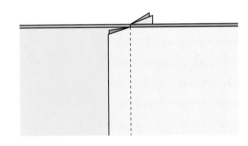

rotary cutting

Let me start by being extremely honest: I didn't know what the heck a rotary cutter was until *after* I had made a handful of quilts. That's right—I cut those bad boys out all by hand, and of course they were full of character (and inaccurate cuts with unmatched seams). But then I discovered rotary cutters, clear acrylic rulers, and self-healing cutting mats—also known as some of the most basic tools for quiltmaking. A rotary cutter looks like a pizza cutter, only it's just for fabric. (Sorry husbands.) Clear acrylic rulers come in many different shapes and sizes, and they're generally marked in ⅛" intervals, making it easy to measure fabric. Self-healing cutting mats are a godsend to quilters; they protect your table from the rotary-cutter blade. Like rulers, they come in many different shapes and sizes. Cutting mats are made from a thick, self-healing material that makes them very resilient to frequent use. Your cutting mat should be marked with easily read numbers and grid lines. I recommend using a 6" x 24" ruler and an 18" x 24" cutting mat.

rotary-cutting tips

⊛ Blades are sharp, so be careful.

⊛ Cut from a standing position.

⊛ Always cut away from yourself.

⊛ Measure twice, cut once.

To square up your fabric, fold the fabric in half and line up the selvages. Place the fabric on your cutting mat. Place a square ruler along the folded edge of your fabric, and then align the right edge of a long ruler with the square ruler, just covering the uneven raw edges as shown. Remove the square ruler and use your rotary cutter to straighten the edge of the fabric, making sure you're cutting through both layers.

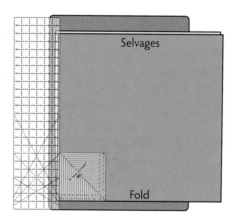

Many projects in this book instruct you to cut a strip of fabric, and then crosscut it into rectangles and squares. To do this, cut strips the required width, and then trim the selvage ends of the strip. Align the desired measurement on the ruler with the trimmed end of the strip and cut a square or rectangle.

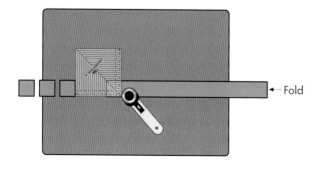

machine piecing

Craftsmanship in a quilt is something to strive for. We all want a quilt we can be proud of, right? After accurate cutting, a precise and consistent ¼" seam allowance is what can make or break a quilting project. If your sewing machine has a ¼" foot, you'll find it much easier to maintain accuracy in your piecing. If your machine isn't equipped with this foot, never fear—it's easy to find the perfect ¼"-wide seam allowance. Promise!

A simple way to create a ¼" seam allowance is by changing the position of the needle on your machine. On a scrap of fabric, sew a line of stitches; then measure the distance from your stitches to the raw edge of your fabric. Stitch, measure, and stitch again until you've found a perfect ¼"-wide seam allowance. You can also measure and place a piece of tape a ¼" to the right of the machine needle, and then use the edge of the tape as a piecing guide.

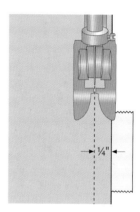

making half-square-triangle units

Some of the quilts in this book require half-square-triangle units. The following method can save effort when it comes to piecing the units.

The basic math for creating these units is to start with squares that are ⅞" larger than the desired finished size of the half-square-triangle unit. For example, if you need a half-square-triangle unit that is 3" finished, you'll start with 3⅞" squares.

1. You'll need two squares of fabric, one print and one solid or one dark and one light.

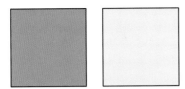

Finished size + ⅞" = square cut size

2. Draw a line from corner to corner on the wrong side of the lightest square.

3. Place the squares right sides together and stitch ¼" from each side of the drawn line. Cut the squares apart on drawn line.

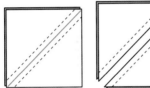

4. Press the seam allowances toward the darker fabric. Trim the dog ears. This process will make two half-square-triangle units.

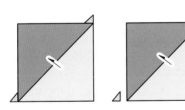

sewing strips

To make strip sets, start by joining two strips along their long edges. Repeat, and then sew the strip pairs together to form a strip set. When sewing the strip pairs together, sew from the opposite end to help avoid distortion in your strip set. (Arrows indicate stitching directions.)

borders

When you've finished assembling the center of your quilt, it's time to add borders, if applicable. The instructions for each quilt in this book will give you the cutting measurements for the borders. However, since your cutting and piecing may have created some slight variations in the center dimensions of your quilt, you should always measure your quilt top before cutting your borders.

1. Measure the length of the quilt top through the center and along both outer edges. If the measurements differ, calculate the average by adding the three measurements together and dividing by three. Cut two border strips to the length determined, piecing as necessary. Mark or pin the center of the border strips and the center of the sides of the quilt top.

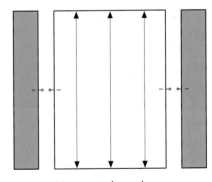

Measure in three places.
Mark centers.

2. With right sides together, Pin the border strips to the sides of the quilt, matching the centers and ends. Pin and sew the side borders to the quilt. Press the seam allowances toward the border strips.

3. Repeat the process for the top and bottom borders, measuring across the side borders you just added when determining the quilt width.

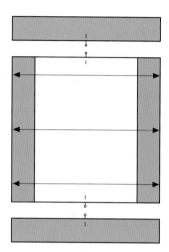

Measure in three places.
Mark centers.

layering and basting

The backing should be at least 4" larger than your quilt top (2" on all sides). To make a simple quilt back, remove the selvages and sew the backing pieces together with a ½"-wide seam allowance. Press the seam allowances open.

Lay the backing, wrong side up, on a clean, flat surface. Anchor the backing in place with masking tape. The backing should be taut, but not stretched out of shape. Center the batting over the backing, smoothing out any wrinkles. Then center the quilt top, right side up, over the batting, carefully smoothing out any wrinkles.

To baste for machine quilting, beginning in the center and working your way out, place safety pins 3" to 4" apart to hold the three layers together.

If you plan to send your quilt to a professional long-arm quilter, check with the quilter before preparing your backing. You probably don't need to baste the layers.

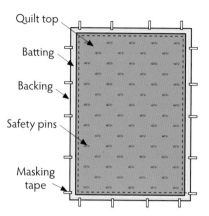

Quilt top
Batting
Backing
Safety pins
Masking tape

quilting

Whether it's hand quilting, machine quilting, or professional long-arm machine quilting, the quilting really enhances the design of your quilt. The quilts shown in this book were all quilted by a long-arm machine quilter, but I do enjoy using my machine to quilt smaller projects like table runners, baby quilts, and lap quilts. Hand quilting seems to be a lost art, but I certainly appreciate the time and effort it takes. Plus it's drop-dead gorgeous. Machine quilting takes a little practice, but I think the best way to ease into machine quilting is by using your machine's walking foot and stitching straight lines using your block seam lines as guides. Once you're comfortable with that, move on to using an open-toe embroidery foot (or darning foot) and try your hand at some free-motion quilting.

binding

Think of binding like the cherry on top of a sundae . . . it just completes your quilt. All of the quilts in this book are bound using double-fold straight-of-grain binding, which means the binding strips are cut along the grain of the fabric, *not* at a 45° angle to the grain (or bias) of the fabric.

Preparing the Binding

Each pattern in this book will tell you the number of binding strips required. While a lot of quilters cut 2½"-wide bindings strips, I choose to cut mine 2¼" wide. All of the patterns in this book reflect my cutting preference, but feel free to experiment with various widths until you find your favorite.

1. With right sides together, overlap the strips at a 90° (right) angle and stitch across the corner to make one continuous strip. Trim the excess fabric, leaving a ¼"-wide seam allowance. Press the seam allowances open.

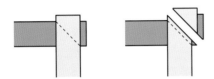

2. Fold the binding strip in half lengthwise, wrong sides together, and press. I use a little spray starch when pressing the binding. I think it makes the binding easier to manipulate.

Fold line

use a walking foot

A walking foot will be your very best friend when attaching binding. A walking foot's sole purpose in life is to ensure that all layers of your quilt move through your machine's feed dogs at the exact same time.

Sewing the Binding

1. Trim the batting and backing even with quilt-top edges. Starting in the center on one side of the quilt, align the raw edges of the strip with the raw edges of the quilt. Leaving an 8" tail and using a ¼" seam allowance, stitch the binding to the quilt, sewing through all the layers. Stop sewing ¼" from the corner. Backstitch one stitch, pivot the quilt one quarter turn, and sew

another stitch. Remove the quilt from the sewing machine and clip the threads.

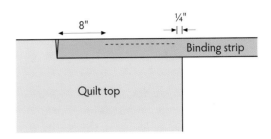

8"   ¼"

Binding strip

Quilt top

2. Fold the binding up and away from the quilt, making a 45° angle fold; finger-press. Keeping the fold in place, bring the binding back down onto itself, even with the edge of the quilt. Start stitching again at the fold, sewing through all the layers.

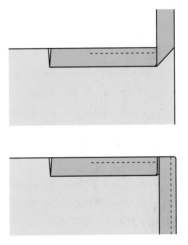

3. Continue around the quilt, repeating the process at each corner. Stop stitching about 8" from where you began and remove your quilt from the sewing machine. Place your quilt on a flat surface and overlap the end of the binding on top of the beginning binding. Mark the end where it overlaps the beginning by ½" and trim the excess.

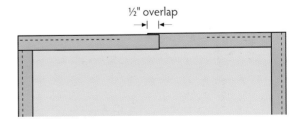

½" overlap

4. Unfold both sides of the binding and place the ends right sides together. Sew the ends together using a ¼"-wide seam allowance. Finger-press the seam allowances open. Refold the binding and finish stitching it to the edge of your quilt.

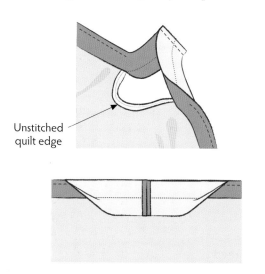

Unstitched quilt edge

5. Fold the binding around to the back of the quilt and use binding clips to hold it in place. Hand stitch the binding in place so that the folded edge covers the row of machine stitching. When you reach a corner, fold a miter in the binding. Take a stitch or two in the miter to secure it. Continue in the same manner, neatly mitering each corner.

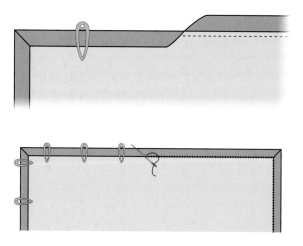

labeling your quilts

A quilt label is like potato salad . . . everyone has her own way of making it.

Let me start by saying that there's no wrong way to label a quilt. Some people like detailed labels, others like ones that are more simplistic, and still others don't even label their quilts at all.

There are several ways to make and attach labels. While I prefer more of a handmade look, others prefer a more computerized, professional feel. I like to sew my labels on by hand. It makes me feel connected to my great-grandmothers.

For a handmade label, use a solid piece of fabric, fuse a piece of fusible web to the wrong side for stability, and then write your message using a fine-point permanent marker, such as a Pigma pen.

When my label is complete, I fuse it in place on the back of the quilt and stitch around the perimeter by hand using a running stitch and cotton thread for that handmade touch. If you'd like, you can apply seam sealant to the raw edges to prevent fraying.

Whether you choose to write on your quilt labels by hand or by computer, know that generations from now, someone can relive a momentous occasion in their ancestor's life.

acknowledgments

This is a platform in which I do not stand alone. Many people helped this book become a reality, and for that, I thank you all.

To my husband, Shane: Not only are you always supportive, you fuel my crazy desire to create in more ways than I could have imagined. Thank you for your patience, your voice of reason, and for not minding dirty socks every now and then.

To my siblings, Zachary, Whitney, and Sean: Y'all amaze me with your constant encouragement and by spurring me along whether you think I'm in over my head or not. Phone five, well, book five!

To my parents and grandparents: I've always been creative and I appreciate y'all letting me explore my creativity.

To Julie Herman: You held my hand and never let go. I'd be lost without you. And I owe you a truckload of M&M's.

To Molly Culley: You treated this book like your own. Thanks for being my wingman.

To my many helping hands: Lani Padilla, Jennifer Blosser, Vanessa Christenson, KarrieLyne Winters, Ashleigh Kolasky, Jamie Faris, Amanda Nelson, and Marci Henry. Every single one of y'all helped make this book possible. I'm truly thankful for every second of help given. Pinky swear.

To my long-arm quilter, Darla Padilla: You never cease to amaze me by bringing my quilts to life. I treasure you (and your APQS Millenium) with all of my heart.

A very special thanks to the wonderful fabric companies that generously donated the yummy fabrics for the quilts in this book: Lissa Alexander and Moda Fabrics; Allie Heath and Robert Kaufman Fabrics; Jamie Acuri and Dear Stella Fabrics; and Pat Bravo and Art Gallery Fabrics.

To the fine folks at Martingale: Karen Burns, Karen Soltys, Cathy Reitan, Sheila Ryan, Nancy Mahoney, and Brent Kane. Thank you for loving my idea and making it come to life. You're the best of the best. I mean it.

And last, but certainly not least, my blog readers: Y'all rock my socks off. And often. Thank you. XO.

about the author

Rachel was born and raised in northern Georgia. She grew up in communities where family held a strong bond, and the influence of her elders and family members led her to a niche in quilting.

When not busy piecing fabrics and designing patterns, Rachel has committed herself to becoming a traditional quilter with a modern twist. She travels far and wide for ideas and inspiration, teaching others the finesse that is quilting.

She and her husband, Shane, currently reside near Cleveland, Ohio, and have four beautiful children in which they invest their time and love.

In her spare time, Rachel loves to research her family's historical records and delve into the rich tapestry of her genealogy. She adores brisk fall weather, and especially enjoys Starbucks coffee from the sidelines of her husband's football games, where she watches him coach.

Find out more about Rachel's adventures and all things quilting by following her blog at www.psiquilt.com.